Call
Nothing
Small

Mary Langford

Preface

I offer to you this collection of articles written over the past several years for publication in *Entre' Nous,* the monthly newsletter of the Evangeline Baptist Association of Louisiana. I usually wrote about some seemingly small event in my life, maybe just something I saw or read, a chance remark or memory which God used to speak to me. There are no big revelations here, just a record of what I heard His still, small voice say. I had difficulty deciding on a title for the collection until one day in my devotional reading in Streams in the Desert I came across this sentence, attributed only to C.H.P.: "God wants us more and more to see Him in everything, and to call nothing small if it bears us His message." I do believe that God is always speaking, and I am trying to train myself to be ever alert to what He is saying. Here I share with you some of what He has communicated to me through nature, travel, family, difficulties, my computer, special days and in other ways.

Mary Langford
March, 2010
Lafayette, LA

May you be aware
each day of This
word to you –
Mary L.

Acknowledgment

My gratitude to Tami Luke for her lovely pen and ink illustrations. Special thanks to Bert Langley, Director of Missions for the Evangeline Baptist Association, and to the Association office staff: Elizabeth Langley, Debbie Jeffreys and Becky Primeaux for their invaluable help. My daughter Devra Langford was of great assistance in bringing the project to completion. And always, my appreciation for my husband Don's biased and unwavering belief in me and in the value of my writing.

Mary Langford

Table of Contents

Difficulties

Special Days

My Computer

Other Ways

Nature

Blanket of Snow

$\mathcal{I}$ have just returned from a visit to family members in Chicago. The first morning I was there, I made my coffee as usual and took my mug to the front window which faces a park. I opened the blinds to a splendid sight! While we slept, snow had quietly fallen and now lay inches thick over everything in sight. The street, the sidewalk, cars, trees, bushes, roofs of houses all sat silent under a cold white coverlet. The ball field in the park was quiet under its smooth blanket. The swings, slide and climbing frame held white piles as if a giant box of powdered sugar had been spilled over them. No footprint, tire track, or any sign of trespassing marred the beautiful scene.

I have continued to remember this perfect picture since I returned home, and the Lord has coupled it in my mind with that powerful promise in Isaiah 1:18: *"Come now and let us reason together . . . Though your sins be as scarlet, they shall be as white as snow. . ."*

Yesterday in my office I met with a young couple who are hoping to rebuild their relationship. He was unfaithful to her, but seems truly repentant. She wants to forgive him, but finds it hard to trust. This often happens in human relationships. We hurt and betray each other. We find it difficult to begin anew and believe in someone again. With God's help, it can be done. He is the source of forgiveness and of second chances. He can help us to cover past sins and hurts in our own lives and in the lives of others with the snow-white blanket of His love.

The Watchful Gardener

The sun is shining, a warm wind plays among the trees, and everything that blooms in spring is shouting, "Hallelujah! Look at me!" Bradford pear trees hold their perfectly shaped white bouquets aloft. Huge old azalea bushes display their full-skirted dresses of fuchsia, coral, pink and white. Redbud trees lift their rosy branches in praise and exhilaration. The Japanese Magnolia gloriously announced the season and then was gone. White blossomed Bridal Veil branches drape and sway in the breeze. It has happened again, so many times, yet ever new—spring has arrived!

And yet, not quite everything is celebrating. On a trellis behind our mailbox grows a vine which is glorious in early summer, with a healthy growth of dark green leaves, small golden flowers, and red wing-shaped seed pods. Every winter when it is dry and bare, I prune it quite severely, feeling bad that I leave it with grey, stubby fingers where its graceful branches used to be. So far, it has always come back to offer its butterfly-like blossoms again for our enjoyment. This year, however, it had us a bit worried. My husband came in the door saying, "You don't think the mailbox vine is dead, do you? I don't see any new growth on it." When I went out for my walk, I stopped to carefully examine the plant. At first, I agreed with my resident yard man's observation. But as I continued to look, I could see here and there just the tiniest sprouts of green, minute tips that signaled life and gave a promise of what is to come. I am confidant that we will enjoy its red and gold glory again.

But I am going to watch it closely while it makes a come-back.

Even while I was inspecting the vine, I had the thought that maybe I had caught just a glimpse of the way the Master Gardener watches with concern the life of one of His children who has undergone severe pruning. Since then, I've thought of those among us, maybe even reading this, who have recently endured a great loss or hurt or disappointment. I'm aware that some are not even able to enjoy the beauty of the new season because of life-threatening illness, or fear of what may be ahead. To any such ones, may I say that God has ordained that spring will follow winter and that the dry, pruned vine will put forth new growth. He overcame death and came forth from the tomb by His own power. And the scripture says He has placed this same power in those who are His. You can trust Him to bring you through the dark time into His light and to make of your life a thing of beauty and something that will honor Him.

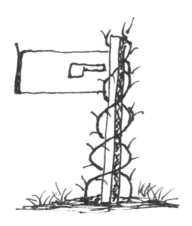

Pleasing Fruit

$\mathcal{I}$ am a summer person. Although I haven't been in school for a long time, I still have a sense of a little more freedom in summer, a feeling of potential holiday. One thing I like best about summer is the abundance of fresh produce that is available. A supper of yellow squash, green beans, and new potatoes along with slices of luscious red homegrown tomatoes and hot cornbread can take me right back to carefree summer visits at my grandmother's house.

Ah, and then there's the fruit. At my house I count summer prosperity in terms of how many kinds of fruit I have on hand. One early morning I picked big juicy blackberries which went into a scrumptious cobbler that night. A friend shared her bounty of crunchy little Bartlett pears because they had so many the tree branches were breaking. Another friend brought beautiful blueberries which enhance our salads and desserts. My husband and I felt rich when we came home with two buckets of figs from another friend's trees. Someone else gave us Ruston peaches. Surely their sweet, gold goodness was one of God's best ideas. And I know He is pleased when we enjoy and revel in all these things He created for our nourishment and pleasure.

His word speaks of other fruit that He can produce in us, fruit that knows no special season and that will bless all those around us. Every day I deal with people who are trying very hard on their own to deal with anger toward an abusive parent, resentment because of an injustice, anxiety over possible events, impatience with rowdy children, lack of discipline in personal habits, or unkindness from a neighbor or co-worker. I try to share with them what I am attempting to do in my own life, which is to open myself to the teaching and discipline of a loving Father who is able to produce in me an ongoing harvest of fruit which delights Him even more than fresh figs and summer squash.

"But the fruit of the Spirit is love, joy peace, patience, kindness, goodness, faithfulness, gentleness, self-control..." Gal. 5:22-23a

The Nautilus

Summer has officially ended, and we are feeling those first little teases of approaching fall in the air. I bade farewell to summer by taking my annual trip to the beach with long-time friends. As always, I enjoyed every minute of our walking, talking, laughing, eating, sharing and praying together, but this year God topped it off with a special blessing. Some time ago I became intrigued by a bit of information I learned about the creature known as the Chambered Nautilus. Since then, I have been wishing for a nautilus shell, and this year at the beach I was able to buy one to bring home. I'm looking for the perfect place and way to display its pearly, iridescent beauty.

But why is this particular seashell so important to me? Thought you'd never ask. First of all, it is thought to have housed one of the earth's oldest living species of sea life, kin to the octopus and squid, sort of a living fossil. The thing that first caught my attention, however, is that this ugly, slow-moving creature starts life in a very small space inside the shell and as it grows, it builds a new, larger chamber into which it moves, lining it with pearlised rainbow walls. When it moves into the new space, it seals the old chamber behind it. Guided by an inborn plan, the nautilus forms a perfect logarithmic spiral as it grows, builds, and moves, providing a wonderful example of growth outward from the center.

There is much more to be said about the Chambered Nautilus, but probably you now understand why I want to have one which I can look at often for the sake of the analogies I can draw from its sluggish, yet amazing, life. Like this ancient animal, I want to be ever growing, expanding my horizons, moving forward spiritually, emotionally and relationally. As I occupy the space where I am at present, I hope to fill its "walls" with a beauty that will be an honor to my Creator and will uplift those who occupy the space with me. When I move ahead, I need to close the door behind me, not resting on past successes, nor remembering past defeats or hurts. And most of all, I need to remember that God has a perfect plan for my life which has little to do with what I possess or achieve, but all to do with allowing Him to grow me from the center outward. Maybe this is why God has left the Chambered Nautilus around for such a long time.

Under the Snow

$\mathcal{I}$ think it's been a while since I've written about my grandson, so brace yourselves, because now I have two! Little Jake Walker was born in Chicago on December 2, and I went up a week later to welcome him and help to get him off to a good start with lots of holding and rocking.

Two days after I arrived, Chicago experienced one of the worst blizzards the city has seen in many years. I was there for three weeks, never saw the temperature above 25, and watched day by day as snow piled on snow. From the front window of my daughter's house I could see the park where I had played with my grandson in summer. The benches and playground equipment were barely visible beneath piles of snow. The rose bushes in their back yard were buried beneath the heavy white blanket that made the green grass only a memory.

Experiencing all that made it difficult to believe that anything could still be alive under all that whiteness, in such bitter cold. Yet, I know that by summer the park will be full of sunshine and children, the roses will be blooming, and the grass will need to be mowed. I know that because I have lived through lots of winters that have become summers.

The same kind of process happens in our lives also. We sometimes have long periods which seem to be barren, cold, and empty. We pray, we wait, we watch, and we say that nothing is happening. In fact, something is happening; we just can't see it yet. He is always at work for a time   before we see the results of the work. Like the grass and the roses that wait beneath the snow, being prepared for spring's growth and beauty, our loving Father is preparing our next blessing or adventure. We must trust Him and say with the poet, "If winter comes, can spring be far behind?"

Better still, in those times when we are not able to see God's activity, let's remember Paul's words in 2 Corinthians 14:16-18 – *"Therefore we do not lose heart. Though outwardly we are wasting away, yet inwardly we are being renewed day by day. For our light and momentary troubles are achieving for us an eternal glory that far outweighs them all. So we fix our eyes not on what is seen, but on what is unseen. For what is seen is temporary, but what is unseen is eternal."*

An Audience of One

The Lord and I recently has a conversation about a tree. Not an audible conversation, you understand, at least not His part of it, but a very clear communication nonetheless. Each late winter season, a tree in an adjacent back yard bursts into full bloom. I'm not sure what kind of tree it is. It isn't the shape of a Bradford pear, and its blossoms are too small to be a dogwood. Whatever kind of tree it is, it is magnificent, a huge bouquet of white flowers, and I have a perfect view of it from my bathroom window.

The point I brought up to the Lord was that it is a shame that so few people can even see the tree or know it's there. The house in that yard is unoccupied, and the lot just behind it is empty too, leaving just me and a neighbor on one side to enjoy the abundant snowy blossoms. I remarked to my Father, the Great Gardener, that it seemed too bad for so much beauty to be visible to so few.

He agreed with me, but then very clearly within me I heard Him say, *"I'm glad you like the tree; I knew you would. And I'm glad you think of Me when you see it. But don't worry that its beauty is wasted. I see it and it pleases Me in every way. I enjoy every leaf and every flower on it. It is a perfect example of one of My creations which is doing to the utmost what I intended it should do. Without a word, in an almost unseen place, it follows My plan*

completely. Its only purpose is to bring glory to Me.
Every day I smile as I receive its voiceless praise." And I
said no more.

Hummingbirds in the Storm

Every August we clean the hummingbird feeders, fill them with sweet, tempting liquid and hang them near a window so we can watch the tiny little birds who stop to feed on their way to Mexico or South America. This year they seemed to especially appreciate what we had to offer, as we had more little hungry visitors than in years past. We never got tired of watching them as they would come zooming in to the red feeding stations, stick their needle-like beaks into the openings and drink their fill, all the while fluttering their wings into a blur. As before, we noticed that, tiny as they are, they are very fierce and territorial, chasing away others of their kind who want to dine at the same feeder. Then we saw that as the weeks went by, they seemed to sense the shortness of time and became less selfish, so that we observed three or four sharing the same feeder. The most amazing thing we saw was during Lili when one or two of the little birds braved the hurricane winds and rain, and defying all logic, came back for nourishment at the one sure source they knew.

During the storm, we sat inside without electricity or running water and watched shingles blow off our roof and limbs break off the trees. I've been through one tornado, many typhoons, and several hurricanes, so I wasn't afraid, but certainly was impressed again with what happens when the powers of nature are unleashed. Like our governor and so many others, I also gave credit to God for exerting

His power at a crucial time and saving our area from worse destruction.

Soon after the storm had abated, I received a call asking me to help at the Red Cross center as a mental health worker. For the next ten days or so I spent part or all of the days listening to stories of people who had lost almost everything. Trees fell in on their houses, clothes and bedding were soaked and mildewed, food was spoiled. They stood in long lines for hours to ask for vouchers for diapers, school uniforms, and food. Most of them had been needy before Lili, and their faces told of their desperation as they struggled to find a bridge between their loss and a new beginning. Over and over as I sat with them and heard their needs and concerns, I noticed that their list ended with, "But thank God, we're still alive," or "Thank God, He protected us." Many of these dear people said to me quietly, "I've been through hard things before. God will see me through this too." During and after a storm of any kind, we need to brave the winds of discouragement and find hope and sustenance in the one sure Source we know.

The Pear Tree

We were more fortunate than many in terms of damage caused by the recent hurricanes. One loss I note each time I return home, however, is that a third of my favorite tree was ripped away by Rita. Several years ago my husband and I planted the Bradford pear beside our driveway, and have enjoyed watching it grow and perform in every season. In spring it covers itself in frothy white blossoms. In summer its bright green leaves stir in the breeze like little fans. And in the fall those leaves change to a beautiful burnt red before dropping off to display in winter the tree's bare limbs forming a perfectly curved shape.

But now my special tree has been wounded. Its shape is no longer perfect, and gashes can been seen near the trunk where its limbs were torn away. Ever since the storm, I have noticed these changes every time I pass my leafy friend. Imagine my surprise when I noticed about a week ago that the Bradford pear was beginning to bloom! It's supposed to bloom in the spring, but here it is in October, bursting with clusters of white flowers. I'm guessing the explanation is the warm fall we've had, or maybe the trauma of the storms, but whatever the reason, my tree seems to be shouting a lesson to me. I hear it saying, "I may be broken, but I can still fulfill my purpose. I can still produce beauty. I can still bless those who pass by. I can still point them to the One who made me and sustains me."

I often counsel with people who have suffered great wounds of loss, abuse, neglect, betrayal or physical suffering. Many times they think, talk and feel like victims. I try to help them to move from seeing themselves that way to viewing themselves as survivors, and then as over-comers and victors. I wish they could all come to see my favorite tree. Maybe if they saw the snowy, out-of-season blossoms surrounding the emptiness where limbs once grew, they too would hear the message of my beloved, broken, brave and still beautiful Bradford pear.

The Purpose of Pruning

This morning I pruned my rose bushes. I've learned that in South Louisiana they are to be cut back moderately in September and more severely in January. Growing roses is new to me, so I'm learning as I go. I find that my little garden gives me good illustrations for marriage counseling because, like a marriage, it needs to be worked in every day. I'm always needing to weed, spray, trim, feed, or water the plants. I'm glad to do those tasks because of the beautiful flowers that result.

Pruning was hard for me to do the first time. It seemed wrong to cut away healthy growth, leaving blunt, bare bushes to start again. Two things helped: I remembered the passage in John 15 which pictures the Father as the gardener who prunes every branch that bears fruit, that it may bring forth more fruit. Secondly, I saw that the severe trimming in January indeed did result in an abundance of colorful blooms in the spring.

Somewhere we got the notion that if we're good, we'll be blessed. We keep thinking that life is supposed to go smoothly. We forget that some lessons can only be learned through suffering. It may be that some of the hard things that come to us, those things that leave us feeling blunt and vulnerable, will in fact result in more fruit of the kind that pleases the Gardener. Probably He often says to Himself with satisfaction (as I did this morning), *"I pruned My special plants today, now I wait with anticipation to see the fruit that will come forth to honor Me."*

The Cardinal's Mistake

The first time I heard the tapping sound I thought someone was knocking on my back door. When I went to check, I found a beautiful male cardinal flying into the breakfast room window, hitting his beak each time on the pane. Now when I hear the tap-tap-tap, I know the visitor is not at the door, but at the window. He comes every morning, lured, I suppose, by the birdseed feeder. Then, I'm guessing, he is distracted by his own reflection in the window. So he goes after that bird to chase him away. He works at it very hard, flying again and again into the window, banging his beak every time. This morning as I watched him, I thought, "Too bad the thought processes in his little bird brain aren't as brilliant as his gorgeous plumage." I wonder how long it will take him to figure out HE is the "enemy."

As I leave home and head to the counseling office, it occurs to me that we human beings are sometimes not so different from my red-feathered friend. When we are young, we figure out how we need to behave to get what we want or to be safe in the family we're in. Then we usually continue some form of that behavior for the rest of our lives, even though it may no longer be appropriate. The way that works is that the child who gets his way with temper fits grows up to be an adult who controls his or her family by anger.

Other examples come to mind: the person who has a pattern of withdrawing from every conflict, rather than learning to talk things out to a positive solution. Or the one who continues to try to cover old pain with habits which are destructive and ineffective. I have seen women who time after time become involved with men who misuse them, each time convincing themselves it will be different. And men who "max-out" their credit cards month after month, buying expensive grown-up toys that never quite fill up the hole inside them.

Periodically we need to ask ourselves if we need to rethink a pattern or change a habit so we won't be like the red bird who continues to bang his own beak in an ongoing battle against himself.

Spring Break

*D*id you know God goes on Spring Break? I spent last week at the beach for my granddaughter's spring break, and He was there. He rode beside me and kept me awake and alert as I drove the several hundred miles between Lafayette and Gulf Shores. We arrived after dark, and He guided us safely to our rented beach house. Each morning I went for long walks on the sand packed solid by relentless washing of the waters of the Gulf. As the waves crashed in time after time, God said, *"This is a picture of my faithfulness: continual, unchanging."* I saw seagulls standing like feathered sentinels before swooping away in graceful arcs. I was charmed by little sandpipers gathered in chirpy avian conferences or running from the waves on tiny toothpick legs. God watched them too and said, *"I know and care for each one and you are more valuable to Me than they are."*

On my walks I saw a house different from its neighbors. They were all well cared for and painted in lovely pastel shades. In contrast, this house stood high on its wooden pilings, gray and storm-battered, looking seaward through broken windows. Its stairs had been swept away by ferocious wind and water. To me, it represented the destruction of someone's dreams and plans. There God whispered, *"Hard times come, but remember what I told you about my faithfulness."*

One day I watched a father teaching his small son

how to fly a kite. As it rose fitfully into the bright sky, the little boy jumped up and down, cheering and pushing his arms upward, as if he could help the kite to greater heights. God and I smiled, and He said, *"That's what I do in your life and what I want you to do in the lives of others."*

The beach was strewn with broken shells which had once been homes for sea creatures. We collected them, and my daughter used them to make beautiful sand art. We enjoyed the creativity, and the finished projects gave pleasure to others on the beach. I think God liked them too, because I read one morning, *"God is building His kingdom with broken things."*

I tried to pray on all my walks, but on the last day, I was so aware of the warm sun, the blue sky, the cool breeze, and the water, deep green in the distance, gradually paler before throwing itself in foaming whiteness onto the sand. I said to God, "Lord, You know the desires of my heart. Would it be all right today if I just walk full of wonder and thanksgiving for the part of Your creation You are allowing me to enjoy? May I just <u>be</u> and not talk?" And He said, *"I would like that very much."* Make no mistake. God goes on Spring Break.

Left-Overs

$\mathcal{I}$ wish you could see the little garden area at our back door. It is ablaze with bright red and pink geraniums, yellow and lavender chrysanthemums, pink begonias, one colorful croton, and several enormous red and white amaryllises, all blooming under an arch covered by deep red climbing roses. This unlikely color combination came about because I grouped the pots there after winter, not remembering exactly what color everything would be when it bloomed again. This is a flower bed of left-over plants I had last year, but they couldn't be more glorious! To top it off, a pair of cardinals have made a nest (also left-over broken sticks and a plastic bag) among the roses on the arch, so we're able to watch them through our breakfast room window. This small patch of ground and its occupants are bringing me daily delight.

And it has set me to thinking about what God does with left-overs. I know we are always taught to give Him our best and our first-fruits. Of course, that is what I believe we should do. But what about the person whose best has been lost or sinned away? What about the marriage that has sustained the wound of adultery or other deception? Or the teenager who has given too soon that which can only be given once? Or the body and mind affected by substance abuse? Every week I sit in my small office with someone who has only a much-used self to offer to God. And I believe that He is delighted with such a gift. Only He knows what He will bring forth from what yet remains. I think He loves to surprise us with the beauty He produces from unexpected sources. When I look at my little garden plot, at my own life, and at some others that I know about, I'm just sure that God likes left-overs.

Spring After Winter

This week I noticed that the Japanese Magnolia or tulip trees are starting to bloom. Last week their branches were dark and bare. Now they burst with lavender blossoms. During days of rain and nights of temperatures in the 20's, those flowers were silently forming. When I see them, I am reminded that the Lord often works in lives in a similar way. I have lived long enough to know that God is always at work for good, and that often He is at work long before the evidence is visible to us. Recently in the counseling office I have seen some of the manifestations of His quiet work in the hearts and lives of people. A young married couple who were separated have discovered that God's word gives a design for marriage and for their relationship. A mother whose only child died several months ago tells me that she was able to bake a birthday cake for someone else on the day that would have been her child's birthday. A step-mother determines to reach out to a difficult step-son as unto the Lord. A widow says, "I must go on. With God's help, I'll make a life for myself."

How thankful I am to be able to observe the results of the Lord's work in nature and in the human heart and mind. Pray for those who still wait for the visible evidence of what He is doing that we cannot yet see. And enjoy the tulip trees.

Travel

Florida Friends

I've just returned from a trip down memory lane. Not a lane really, but an L-shaped path from Tampa to Ft. Lauderdale, FL. My husband and I had planned the journey as the prequel to a mission trip to Haiti. When strong warnings from the U.S State Department caused us to cancel going to Haiti, we decided to continue with the long-held wish to visit friends and family in Florida. In the week there we enjoyed the white sand beaches, golden sunshine, the waves and blue waters of the Gulf of Mexico and the Atlantic Ocean. We toured museums and a wild-life preserve. We had delicious meals in homes and restaurants. We drove by Donald Trump's home in West Palm Beach.

We did all that and much more, but none of those things were the most memorable part of our trip. The reason we went was to see people who are dear to us, folks with whom we share some history. We had wonderful, uplifting visits with four couples from our past who range in age from the sixties to almost eighty. One pair we met in Israel twenty years ago. The others we've known for much longer, and they shared all or part of our time in Hong Kong. With each one we spent hours reminiscing, laughing, sharing hopes and concerns, and reveling in that comfortable feeling that is brought on by years of shared experiences.

All that was such a blessing in the moment, but more blessing has come as I reflected on those visits. As we went from home to home, my husband and I saw the fulfillment of the promise in scripture. We saw people who dedicated themselves as servants of God when they were young, still serving, still ministering to the needs of others, still trying to patiently love others into God's kingdom. Most of them are dealing with medical problems, but they continue with the work the Lord has given to them. And we saw how God, in every case, has blessed them with lovely places to live and work to do and children who have concern for them. They have positive attitudes and plans for the future. They are trying to eat healthily and exercise. They are readier to serve than to be served. They were such an encouragement to us. Old friends are best. And God is to faithful to those who are His.

What I Heard In Hershey

A few weeks ago my husband and I met friends for a week of vacation in Pennsylvania. The weather was beautiful, and we had a wonderful time touring the many interesting sites in the Hershey/Harrisburg/Lancaster area. Most of you will know that Lancaster is the heart of the Amish country, those self-proclaimed "plain people" who have chosen a simple, devout way of life. Their food, crafts, quilts and farms show their dedication to excellence. South of Lancaster, in Strasbourg, was the main reason for our trip: two Sight and Sound theaters where magnificent Biblical dramas are presented throughout the year. We saw "Abraham and Sarah" and "In the Beginning." In both productions the music, acting, sets, costumes and depiction of great truths were superb. In Harrisburg we spent hours in the National Civil War Museum, being reminded again of the emotional, financial, medical, personal and national cost of that war.

In Hershey we visited the gorgeous Hershey Gardens with its more than seven hundred rose bushes. We spent a lovely morning learning about the amazing Milton Hershey school for underprivileged children. Of course, we toured the Hershey candy factory. As many people have probably done, we rode the little open train through the animated mock-up of the process of making chocolate candy. Here's what I can recall of what happens: first the cocoa beans must be brought from a far country. Then they are cleansed. After that they are broken, ground and roasted. They are pressed and refined. At some point, other important ingredients are added, such as milk and sugar. All this is mixed to just the right flavor and consistency. Then it is poured out and molded into the familiar Hershey products which we all enjoy.

Can you believe that while I was riding that little train, trying to hear the recorded narration over the singing of the mechanical cows, God pointed out to me how very similar the Hershey process is to what He is always doing in the lives of His children? We must first be brought from the far country of sin, then cleansed and broken, pressed and refined. As we grow in Him, His Spirit adds those qualities which make our lives sweeter to Him and to others. He wants us to be willing to be poured out in service to Him and molded into the likeness of His Son. Next time you eat a piece of chocolate candy, think about all that had to happen to it before it got to you, and remember that God wants to do those very things in your life.

Those Who Serve in Far Places

Since my last column I've had some unusual adventures. I've ridden on the back of an elephant in a river and through tribal villages in a primitive oxcart. I've watched silk being made from cocoon to loom and observed artists making beautiful hand-painted umbrellas. I've watched skilled woodcarvers using simple tools to create amazing designs in teak and rosewood. I've eaten strange, exotic fruits and shopped in a crowded bazaar. Can you tell that my husband and I have just returned from Thailand? What a fascinating and memorable trip!

As much as we enjoyed all the unfamiliar flavors, sights and experiences, that was not the most important part of the trip. We went to the other side of the world to meet and give support to a group of missionaries gathered at a location north of Bangkok. I wish you could have been with us to meet those folks. Most of them are young couples with small children. They live in isolated, mainly Muslim, villages in several Asian countries. They work as teachers, veterinarians, language specialists, agriculturalists, physicians, and they are some of the sharpest and most innovative people I have ever encountered. They live among the local people, learn their languages, and become their friends. They try to offer them a better life in terms of both basic and spiritual needs. We felt privileged to be among them and to offer medical and/or counseling help as requested.

Since we've returned, I keep seeing the faces of those special people. I hear again the prayer requests they made. They asked for safety for their children, especially from snakes. They need wisdom to know how to relate to those with whom they live and work. They hope for favor with the government to obtain visas. They are concerned about parents in the States. One young wife is expecting her first child. They live in hard places, and they have given themselves to reach people who may be forever lost without their effort. They need to be lifted up to the Father every day. I hope you already have the habit of praying regularly and in specific ways for missionaries.

One of the Earth's Hard Places

Greetings from Kishinev, Moldova! (Look on the map between Romania and Ukraine.) I'm writing this on March 16, 1999, my fourth day in this capitol city of 800,000 mainly Russian-speaking people. Today, as each morning, I woke to find a thin blanket of new-fallen snow. After breakfast I bundled into all-weather coat, boots, scarf and gloves and went with four other teachers out into the frigid morning to ride the bus to the Seminary where we have come to teach for two weeks. It is located on the 11th floor of a building which is dirty, drafty, and in disrepair. Two small flats have been remodeled and combined to house the four-year school which now has 42 students. Among their number are a former KGB agent, a former prostitute, and many who are the only Christian in their family.

The elevator is creaky, unreliable, and has no light, so we choose to walk up the 11 flights of stairs. Once there, I catch my breath and change into house-shoes (the custom here). Then I go into a small classroom where I spend the morning teaching fourth year students about pre-marital and marital counseling. They are bright, dedicated young men who speak good English with a charming Russian accent. Their ministry will place them against their culture.

For lunch I had some doughy sort of dumplings with a few small pieces of beef prepared in the school's tiny kitchen. Then I had a counseling session with one of the female students. After that I bundled up again, went down the 11 flights of stairs (so much easier), and walked back home the mile uphill through a lightly falling snow.

How grateful I am to be in this cold gray place to have a small part in training ministers to serve the same Lord who guides and blesses the work in Acadiana. Continue to pray for me and for them.

Believers in Moldova

Now I know a man who gets up every morning at 4:00 AM to walk for miles and pray for those who live in his city. He is a dreamer and visionary whom God has used to grow a ten-person Bible study into an 800 member church in five years. I know a seminary student who earns his tuition by sleeping on the floor to be the school's night watchman. He is from a village outside the capital city and is the only Christian in his family. His eyes fill with tears when he speaks of his grandmother who doesn't know Jesus.

Then there's Lina who has wild and curly black hair and sparkling eyes. She attends Moldova Bible Seminary to learn to work with children, but already she is able to hold the attention of a large group of them as she tells them the stories all children need to hear.

I want you to know Eugene, blond and blue-eyed, a young man of many talents. He is assistant to the pastor and seminary director. He translates every sermon and the counseling afterwards. He leads the praise and worship at the beginning of the service. He will graduate from seminary in May. He lives with and cares for his mother who is a Jewess and an alcoholic.

Another seminary student is Elena, who was a prostitute, but who came to the Lord by reading a Gideon Bible in a hotel room. Men from her old life continue to try to lure her back.

And there's Ludmilla, who works each day in the small kitchen at the seminary, cooking morning snacks and a noon meal for the students. She asks for help in knowing how to deal with her young children.

Meet Slavok, hulking and quiet, a former police officer who now spends his days visiting prisons and hospitals winning people to the Lord.

Because of God's provision and your prayer support, I came to know these Christians and more in Kishinev, Moldova, one of the world's smallest and poorest countries, and my life is richer for it. They are our brothers and sisters. Choose one of them to pray for.

A Special Door

$\mathcal{I}$n celebration of our fifty years together, Don and I took a long-dreamed-of trip to Ireland. Except for the poor exchange rate between the Euro and the US dollar, it was all we had hoped for. We spent eight days soaking in the lush greenness, the gorgeous flowers, the unexpected sunshine, the pastures of wooly sheep. We delighted in the friendliness of the people and the lovely lilt to their speech. We climbed to the top of Blarney Castle and watched others lie down and bend backward to kiss the Blarney Stone. We explored the roofless, but amazing, Rock of Cashel, the castle where St. Patrick baptized the first high king of Ireland in 450 A.D. We had a cheese, crackers and fruit lunch on a bench overlooking the spot where John Wesley preached an outdoor sermon in 1785. In the same little town we found a small church which has been in constant use for over 1400 years. We stood in awe as the sun streamed through the richness of its beautiful stained glass windows.

In Dublin we spent most of the morning at Trinity College examining the marvelous display of the Book of Kells, the books of scripture so painstakingly copied and illustrated by monks who devoted their entire lives to the task and who considered every line they wrote to be an act of worship. On Sunday morning we went to the famous St. Patrick's Cathedral. A special section of the sanctuary was set aside for prayer and we made use of it, leaving our written requests, too, in the book provided. Just before leaving, we heard the angelic sound of the choir boys in rehearsal.

One of the most memorable sights in that grand old church was an old, thick, dark door standing upright in a stone base. It was the Door of Reconciliation. It seems that two Irish clans had battled each other for decades and many of their family members had died to keep animosity alive. Finally, one brave man went to the door of the other clan leader and offered peace. Not trusting him, they refused to open the door. At last, he took his axe and hacked a hole in the door through which he extended his weaponless hand. And after all those years of fighting, reconciliation took place. I keep thinking about how courageous and determined that man was. And I think of the number of people I see who are holding grudges, nursing old hurts, not speaking to others, protecting their rights. I wish they could see that big old door with a hole in it. Paul wrote, *"All this is from God, who reconciled us to himself through Christ and gave us the ministry of reconciliation."* (2 Cor. 5:18)

A Joyful Journey

$\mathcal{I}$ have recently returned from a trip that was truly a taste of heaven! One of the bonuses in my life is that my husband and I help to provide member care for a group of missionaries who serve in various countries in Asia. Most of this care is done by telephone, e-mail, fax or meeting with them when they are in the U.S. Every three years, however, they gather at a location in the foothills of the mountains above Chiang Mai, Thailand, and they invite us to join them there. Although the weather is very hot, the setting is beautiful with its teak buildings and lush landscape. With this stimulating group who had come from China, India, Indonesia, Malaysia, Singapore and Thailand, we sang, worshipped, laughed, enjoyed luscious and bountiful meals, and heard stories of wonderful things that God is doing in the places where they live and work. Many of the group had just come from the heart-rending tsunami scenes and recovery efforts. Don and I met with a number of the missionaries regarding medical and/or counseling needs, which was our basic purpose for being there. But we were encouraged and invigorated again by the energy, the creativity and the intelligence of these outstanding people who are dedicated to spreading the gospel in Asia.

Now that would have been enough, wouldn't it? But the Lord had even more in store! After we left Thailand, He allowed us to go back to Hong Kong to visit the people and places that became so dear to us in the twenty-six years we lived and worked there. The city itself is burgeoning, with new buildings going up everywhere. The standard of living is obviously higher than before. But most encouraging to us were the number of Christian friends of former years we found still in their places in the churches and community, still serving, still faithful. A taste of heaven was being able to put our arms around, share a meal with, share our lives again with special people who are still dear to us after so many years apart. Each day there was a blessing and a benediction. We have returned home full of more thanksgiving than we can express.

A Sculpture Speaks

𝒯his has been my year for museums, as my husband and I have toured museums in Washington, Oregon, Pennsylvania, New Orleans and elsewhere. At this point, I must urge you to visit the World War II museum in New Orleans if you have not done so. Take your children and your grandchildren, as it is a war most of them know very little about. I'm sure you will come away, as I did, with a renewed sense of gratitude to those who paid such a great price for the freedom and privileges we enjoy as Americans.

I felt that way too as we made our way through the National Civil War museum in Harrisburg, Pennsylvania. This carefully planned and constructed, still-new museum is located on a hill near the downtown area of Pennsylvania's capitol city. One is struck immediately by the obvious dedication to detail and to fair documentation of America's bloodiest war. Every aspect of the conflict is included: uniforms, food, music, weapons, medical care and more. We walked out with indelible impressions of the financial, emotional, physical, social and national cost of that time in our history.

What I remember most, however, is what greeted us before we ever went inside the building. On a dais in front of the entrance is a very special bronze sculpture which commemorates one of the most heroic acts of the tragic four-year period of the Civil War. A plaque tells the story which took place in a battle in Virginia in December, 1862. Union and Confederate forces faced each other across an open field. The battle raged all day, with the Confederates protected behind a stone wall. By night-fall, over 6000 Union soldiers lay dead or wounded in the falling snow. By the next morning, young Confederate Sergeant Kirkland could no longer bear the cries of the wounded in the near-zero temperature. Gathering as many canteens as he could carry, and risking his life as he did so, he ran out into the field and went from soldier to soldier, giving water and comfort. When the Union commander realized what Sergeant Kirkland was doing, he ordered a cease-fire. Both sides stood silent, watching in awe as the young Rebel soldier moved with compassion among his enemies. The sculpture is a life-like depiction of Sergeant Kirkland kneeling beside a Union soldier, lifting his head to give him a drink from a canteen. The sculpture is named "Moment of Mercy."

How appropriate that this event occurred in December, the time when we celebrate an event not unlike the one I've just described. Since the first human beings, mankind has been at war with God, making ourselves into His enemies. But, at a certain time in history, He heard the cries of distress, the prayers of His people. He gave up all the glories of heaven to be born as a baby, grow as a child, live as a man. He showed us what life was meant to be. Not counting the cost, He gave Himself to give to His enemies the water of life. It was history's greatest Moment of Mercy. This Christmas, let us stand in silent awe. Let us worship and give thanks. In the new year, let us be bearers of living water.

Family

The Economist

$\mathcal{I}$ Am married to the pack rat of the universe. Not just the world. The universe. There would be no way to estimate the amount of stuff he has scavenged from dumpsters, curbside piles, garage sales and Goodwill. In the almost forty-nine years of our marriage, this habit has been an ongoing topic of "discussion" between us. Actually, we agree—up to a point. I also believe in reusing, recycling, not wasting. But I don't think that means we must keep *everything* until the day when its *raison d'être* is revealed.

The problem is that occasionally my husband reaches into his treasure trove and pulls forth exactly what is needed for a repair job or to build something that's needed around our house. Nothing delights him more than reworking an old piece and giving it a new usefulness. I'm also glad when that happens, although I know it weakens my case for an orderly carport. Just recently he patiently and painstakingly put together a small moveable greenhouse which protects our outdoor plants on a south-facing porch. He used some of the old lumber he'd been saving and that I'd been stepping over and fussing about. He, the plants and I are all pleased with the outcome.

Actually, my husband and I are closer together in our thinking than it might seem. As I meet with clients in counseling, many times they are wondering why they are having certain experiences or how they can possibly use some lesson which life has brought to them. I always try to encourage them that God is the Great Economist. He wastes nothing that we give to Him. He looks at us and sees us as we are sometimes—weakened, dulled, set aside—and He envisions what we can be as we give ourselves and our experiences into His masterful hands. I've seen how this works in my own life, and I hope you have evidence of it too.

But, please, if you have something to get rid of, *don't call my husband.* Thanks

Promises, Promises

$\mathcal{L}$ong before the well-known organization came into being, my grandmother was a Promise-Keeper. If she promised me a cake with cherry icing, she made it. If she said she'd make a dress for my favorite doll, she did it. If she told me I could help churn the butter, I could count on it. Once, only once, she promised me a spanking, and to my amazement, she delivered! On her work-worn hand she wore a ring with a rosy stone that I thought was a ruby. She promised it would be mine one day. After her death, it disappeared, but thirty years later it was brought to me, smaller than I remembered, and surely not a ruby, and yet a promise fulfilled.

Recently I've been listening to and reading a plethora of political promises. I've been asking God for wisdom to choose the candidate whose vows are most realistic and most pleasing to Him. I'm hoping I voted for promise-keepers.

Every week I meet with people who are dealing with the aftermath of broken vows, the consequences of neglected commitment. They thought their spouse or friend or relative was a promise-keeper, but that person was not.

In preparation for the Women's Day of Prayer theme "Celebrate the Promises of Christ," I began today to look for His promises in the New Testament. I'm writing them down, so I can remember them and share them with others. There are <u>so</u> many of them, and each one <u>will</u> come to pass. Promises...promises... From the greatest of all Promise-Keepers.

A Special Recipe

$\mathcal{T}$he Lord has had a laugh on me today–and I'm smiling myself. Here's what happened:

My mother has lived with us for eight years, but because of her diminishing memory, judgment, and reasoning power, we are moving her this weekend to a more protected environment. I had some bananas that would not live another day, so I decided to put them out of their misery by making a banana pudding for tonight's dessert. I thought Mother and I could make it together and then I would write a poignant little piece about how she could no longer remember the recipe for the first and simplest dish she taught me to make when I was a little girl.

Into her kitchen I went with my recipe card and brown–speckled bananas. To double-check my theory, I asked "Do you remember what we need?" "Yes," she said, "Less than a cup of sugar." (the recipe says 3/4 cup) "O.K., then what?" "Two tablespoons of flour, two eggs, and two cups of milk." I checked my card. She was right. I heard God chuckle.

She stirred the mixture over the heat until it became thick. I asked, "Do you remember what we do now?" "I think we add 1 tablespoon butter and 1 teaspoon vanilla." Right again. As I poured the hot mixture into a dish layered with vanilla wafers and bananas slices, I thought about how impossible it is to predict what will remain in human memory. I thanked the Lord for His love that never fails, for His word that is eternal and for His mercies that are new every morning and in every season of life.

Make some banana pudding, enjoy it, and pray for my mother during this time of transition. Better memorize that recipe, as it's apparently one of the last things to go.

Book Learning

My husband Don is the sort of person who usually just does what has to be done without giving a lot of thought as to how he feels about it. Whether it's taking out the garbage, working a twelve-hour day at the clinic, or staying with yard work till 10:00 PM., he just digs in and does it without discussion, because it is a necessary job. Recently, however, I noticed that a certain task was different for him. He has moved to a new office with new bookshelves, and we agreed this was the ideal time for him to trim his medical library, getting rid of outdated books or those he no longer uses. As he worked his way through the book boxes, he began saying things like, "This is a hard thing to do," or "I didn't realize what this would be like." Finally, I (the ever-perceptive counselor) heard what he was saying, and encouraged him to tell me why he is finding it so hard to get rid of the books. He replied that many of them are like old friends. Some of them he's had since medical school, they helped to teach him basic information, and their pages are very familiar to him. When he picks up others, he is reminded of certain professors or med-school classmates. Still others call to mind patients through the years who have been helped by what he learned in late-night reading sessions before surgery. Probably hardest of all, this act acknowledges that, although he continues to practice medicine, his days in the operating room are over.

Having said all that, practicality takes over, and he continues to choose the books which must go. Though some are new, others are becoming outdated and need to be used now. They will be given to an institution where they can be used for teaching and will be well cared for. It is comforting to think that their usefulness is not over, just transferred to another location. Don will pass them on because it is the right thing to do.

It occurs to me that this event in our lives is a good example of what I often try to teach people in the counseling office: Our feelings are important and valid and we need to look at them and call them by name. In particular, we need to see how they are affecting our lives and those around us. But we need to base our choices and our actions on what is right, regardless of how we feel. God's word shows us what is right. We all choose every day whether to follow our feelings or His instructions.

Lay Aside the Old

Our Dallas daughter Devra has just spent a long weekend with us. It was our delight to have her and her funny, precious little one with us for those days. Our daughter always comes with a hope and a plan to help "organize" her dad and me. This time she attacked my husband's tie collection. She took all of them off their hooks and set aside those she deemed outdated or otherwise unacceptable. The rest she sorted by color and asked her dad to choose the ones he liked the best. This was all done quickly and with dispatch. The discarded ties were boxed and taken to Goodwill. Because Devra found her dad to be surprisingly compliant through this process, she then started on belts and suspenders. After she left, my husband was so much in the spirit of clearing out that he went through his shoes and gave away several pairs.

I related this incident to a client I saw today who has decided to make some changes, "Nothing big", she says. But as she sees it, she has been living her life for many years in unhealthy ways, bad habits she's held onto too long, like those outdated ties. She's spent a long time waiting for others to be different. Now she is choosing to make positive changes in her own life. Having made this decision, she feels lighter, more focused, more like she is becoming the person God intended her to be.

Paul almost used the closet example when he said *"Lay aside the old self... Be renewed in the spirit of your mind, and put on the new self."* (Ephesians 4:22-24) Our closet-cleaning weekend made me feel great, and I know God is pleased when we are compliant with His desire to clear the negative, unhealthy habits out of our minds and hearts.

My Dad

$\mathcal{M}$ay is my father's birthday month, and June holds Father's Day, so I'm thinking much of my dad, and I'd like to tell you a bit about him. He was born in 1912, the oldest child of a poor Christian couple who lived in a weather-grayed wooden house in a map-dot of a town in east Texas. He worked hard to obtain a college degree and became a teacher. He held a variety of jobs in his lifetime, and finally owned an advertising business, but he never stopped learning, and he never stopped teaching. Mostly, he taught by example, and that is the way I learned so much from him. Because he read to us, I learned to love words and the places they could take me in my imagination. Because he listened to me so patiently, I learned what power there is in giving full attention to another person. My dad had a great curiosity about the world he lived in and wanted to see as much of it as possible. When I have a chance to travel, I think I hear him whisper in my ear, "I'd go if I were you."

Daddy loved people, no matter what size or color, and made friends wherever he went. My two sisters and I never had any doubt about his love for us. His discipline was firm, but not harsh, and usually consisted of a serious talk. We always knew we were special to him; he was expressing that even on his deathbed. Most of all, he loved our mother, serving and caring for her until his heart and body gave out.

My dad loved the Lord, His word, and His church. He left an example of one who spent much time in Bible study and then in sharing what he learned with classes at church and with people in other countries. He poured his life and energy into building up and sustaining the church in which I grew up.

Daddy did all the right things before the "fathering" books were written. He touched, listened, taught, challenged, disciplined, played, led and loved. Because of him, it was easy for me to put my faith in a Heavenly Father who would do all that and more. Join me in giving thanks for your father. Even those who failed in their task taught much. Honor your father if he is living. Thank God for being your perfect, eternal, unchanging Father.

A Super Good Day

When was the last time you had a super good day? And what made it so? Are you like me in often measuring the success of a day by the number of things you are able to mark off your "to-do" list? Recently the assessment of my day was done by a five-year-old, and I've continued to remember what he said.

Here's what happened: I drove to Gulf Shores to join my two grandsons and their parents for a few days at the beach. One of those days I spent alone with the older boy, James. In the morning we sat together on the warm sand by the rhythmic waves and built a castle. We decorated it with bird feathers, gave it a front door made of a large curving seashell and surrounded it with a moat spanned by a driftwood bridge. Next, James wanted to play games: pick-up sticks and our version of dominoes. He won every time, fair and square. Then it was time to swim, first in the outdoor pool, where he met a new playmate, then in the warmer indoor pool. When the playmate left and James was waterlogged, we went back home for a late lunch. Using the pick-up sticks, I taught him the names of their colors in Chinese, promising some ice cream when he said them all right. About this time James said suddenly, "I like this day!" I asked him why, and he named all the fun things we'd done. I agreed that it was indeed a good day. He countered with the words I enjoy remembering, "I think it's a <u>super</u> good day!"

I marked nothing off my list that day, but I count it as a day well spent. Sometimes we need to set our lists aside and just be with someone, just relax and enjoy. I invite you to do that now and then without any guilt. In the warm months ahead I wish for you some <u>super</u> good days!

Family Fun

When you read this, I will be in chilly Chicago welcoming a new grandchild into the world. I'm excited about going to be with my children and grandchildren for a while. And I think they are glad I'm coming. I could hear the pleasure in four-year-old Jake's voice on the phone when he learned I was coming to "sleep over." And eight-year-old James, who has been reading about King Arthur and his Round Table, wants to know if we can watch "Camelot" when I come. The weather is very cold in Chicago now, but I don't care. The house will be full of the noisy activity of two energetic little boys, plus the cries of a newborn. I will do laundry and cook, help with homework, make snacks, read stories, shop for groceries, play games, climb up and down three flights of stairs many times a day. It will be exhausting! And I will love it! I have volunteered to go because I delight in being a part of what's going on in the lives of my children and grandchildren. I want to be one of the first ones to hold that new baby and assure him/her of a love that surrounds, provides for and protects.

Isn't it wonderful to know that the pleasure we have in being with our children is only a mild reflection of our Father's delight in being right in the middle of the events of our lives? Over and over we see scriptural evidence that the Lord longs to be with us, to be invited to share the joys and to help carry the burdens, to assure us of His love and provision. As I counsel people who come to me, I sometimes feel so sad for those who are struggling on their own with a problem or who have entered into a life relationship without giving God an important place in it. When God came to earth, He celebrated weddings, enjoyed eating with those He cared about, wept with friends who grieved, and held little children in His arms. The Perfect One did not hold Himself away from the life events swirling around Him. He participated, with enthusiasm and love. And He lives still, wanting/waiting every day to see who will invite Him into their lives.

My Long-Time Companion

$\mathcal{I}$'ve known my husband Don since he was eighteen years old. I've watched his dark hair turn almost white, the laugh lines become deeper near his eyes and his waistline expand. We've traveled many miles together in all sorts of weather and conveyances in many countries of the world.

We've had heated arguments over some ridiculous things, and then had a lovely time making up. Together we've reared five children, kept a near impossible schedule, dealt with broken bones and broken hearts, adopted Hong Kong as our second home, struggled to learn a foreign language, cared for each of our parents in their last days, and grieved the death of our second son. As I look back over the years since 1956, there are some things I appreciate about my husband: He takes out the trash without having to be asked. He is a hard worker, be it in the clinic or in the yard. He enjoys having visitors in our home and is a thoughtful host. Every morning (Get this, guys) he gets up early, makes the coffee and serves it to me in bed. He encourages me to learn and to grow and to try new things. He trusts me to be sensible about spending. He has been very helpful and generous to my family. When there's a challenge or a difficult task, he stays with it as long as it takes. (Of course, the flip side of that is stubbornness). He's known for careful attention to detail in his work. (Ask him the time; he'll tell you how to make a clock.) He gladly eats anything I put before him, even if he's recently seen it in another form, and always thanks me for the meal. He laughs readily and is always ready to hear or tell a funny story. (Even if I've heard it a hundred times.) He never uses profanity, even when he's angry. He has a lively curiosity about the world around him. (He bought a book on how to make a thatched roof.) He can repair almost anything. He compliments me often, and tells me every day that he loves me. He has been faithful to me for all these years. His faith in God is a vital element of his daily life. Maybe as you've read my list you've seen some traits that remind you of your own spouse. Or maybe you've seen some ideas that you think are worth emulating. Don isn't perfect, but if he were, he couldn't live with me. I know I'm very fortunate the Lord brought us together and has kept us together for more than half a century.

Legacy of Faith

Well, as of January 24, there is a new little soul on this earth. Her name is Ellis Grace Langford. I arrived in Dallas just in time to welcome her and to be among the first to hold her. For two weeks after that, I held her more, rocked her, fed her, burped her, changed her, washed her clothes, sang to her, swaddled her, talked to her and kissed her. I loved being there for her first walk in the stroller, her first ride in the car, her first trip to the pediatrician, her first time to a restaurant. I accompanied her on her very first outing, which was to an art show. (Is my granddaughter cultured, or what?)

As special as all that was for me, I know Ellis won't remember a bit of it. I already love that little girl so much, and she doesn't really even know who I am. Later her mother can show her pictures to prove that I was there for those events, but I want her to know ME. Now what can I do abut that? I am determined to see her as often as possible. I'll continue to do many of the things I've already done for her. When she's older, we can play games, sing songs, and I'll teach her to count in Chinese. But I want her to know ME, so before she was born, I started a little journal that I'm writing just to and for her. In it I'm telling her of the history of people in her family. I'm recounting the thoughts and feelings I had while waiting for her to become one of us.

Most important, I'm telling her about my faith in God and about the way I pray for her. I want her to know me, and I want her to know the most important One in my life. I'll talk with her about these things when I can, but I want her to have it in writing, too, so she can read it when I'm not around.

I share this in the hope that some of you will be encouraged to be sure to make a way to share yourself and your faith with the younger people in your life. You probably take them places, buy them presents, tell them that you love them. But do they know your story, and in particular, how you came to know the Lord and what He means to you? Let's all give this greatest of gifts to those who come behind us.

Balcony People

Two people in my life have been my cheerleaders since the day I was born. One was my dad who died in 1991, speaking words of love and encouragement as long as he was able. The other was his younger sister, Aunt Bobbye, who died on October 9, 2007. She was only six and a half years older than I, and was a care-giver and playmate to me from my earliest years. Together we climbed trees, played in the rain and cut paper dolls from old Sears catalogs. She took me to school with her and on outings with her friends, always making me feel wanted and special. As we grew older, she became my friend and confidant, ever ready to share a story, a laugh, a prayer need. She was beautiful and smart, never too busy to listen, and never ended a conversion without saying, "I love you."

Bobbye was born into a poor family in a town that then and now is just a dot on the map. As a three-pound premature baby in the days before neo-natal hospital units, chances were against her survival. She did survive, however, and set the pattern for many life challenges to come. After high school, Bobbye left her small home town for further training. After her husband's death, she became very respected and successful as a landman in the petroleum industry, a kind of work usually done only by men. She was capable, fair and honest, always keeping her dignity as a woman. She was a wonderful mother and grandmother, an example to all the women in our family of setting a goal, working heard to achieve it, and managing to look classy while she did it.

Space does not allow me to describe all the obstacles Bobbye met and overcame in her lifetime, but she always knew she did not face these things in her own strength. As a little girl in that small Texas town, she had given her life to the Lord, and she relied on Him every step of the way through every financial, emotional and physical challenge. I'm already missing her, but I thank God I know I will see her again. And I thank Him for giving me such a model. I think Bobbye's life could be summed up in the simple words, "She loved others; she trusted God." I invite you to join me in living our lives in that same way.

In Whatsoever State

$\mathcal{I}$n mid-February my husband and I visited his aunt who is in a nursing home in Baton Rouge. This visit was a special one, as it marked her ninety-sixth birthday. She came into the Langford family by way of marriage to my husband's uncle. They met and married in Memphis when he was in medical training and she was a nurse. Her last name was Beasley, so she was dubbed "Bea" by her co-workers, and that's what we've always called her, although her real name is Mary Alice, the same as mine.

I first met Bea more than fifty years ago when she and her husband Carl lived in Ruston where, in spite of severe crippling from an accident, he had an active OB-GYN practice and where they were well-known and respected in the community. I enjoyed visiting in their sprawling ranch-style home on a big shady lot in a lovely up-scale neighborhood. Carl and Bea lived well, traveled extensively, owned fine cars, entertained graciously. Later they bought a lake house where they enjoyed weekends and holidays with friends and family. Finally, Carl retired. They sold the big house in town and moved to the lake. This required a huge downsizing of possessions. Later, they needed to sell the lake house and move back into a rented house in town to be nearer medical help. Again, more disposing and narrowing down. Bea retained her "live well" attitude, even though their circumstances were greatly restricted. When her own sight began to fail and she could no longer care for Carl alone, their children moved them to the nursing home in Baton Rouge where their home consisted of two rooms. Bea could take only a few of her own things; most of the household belongings were dispersed. Then her beloved Carl died. Now she lives in one room with a bed, a chair, a table and a chest. And she said to me, "This is a nice place."

I have continued to think about Bea and what has sustained her through all the changes in her life, and I have come to some conclusions. Her happiness does not depend on things, but on her faith in God and love of others. She does not dwell on losses in the past. She chooses to be content, wherever she is. She is grateful for the smallest of gifts. Isolated as she is, she retains a genuine interest in others and their activities. There is much more, but I'll end by saying I want to be like that Mary Alice Langford when I grow up.

The Little Ones

$\mathcal{B}$efore autumn comes, I must tell you about the most important event of my summer: the birth of our fifth grandchild and second granddaughter. Chloe Laurine Langford entered the world on June 16, weighing nine pounds, six ounces. She has bright eyes and dark hair that stands up like a brush on the back of her head. She is the source of joy and thanksgiving to our son Paul, his wife Jennifer, and our whole family. I'm not sure why they chose the name Chloe, but I learned that Laurine is a special name from my daughter-in-law's family. They are a wonderful group who will be a blessing in her life. Chloe is only two months old, but she is a very fortunate little girl, completely surrounded by those who love her and who are committed to providing all she needs and more. I pray every day for her protection and that she will grow in all ways that are good in God's sight.

One reason I pray that way is because almost every week in the counseling office I see or hear about children who have not been protected, who are not being parented well, who are being adversely affected by events in their home, or who are trying to find a safe place in the battles that are ongoing between their parents. You who read this know these children too, because you are their pastors, their Sunday school leaders, their school teachers. In some cases, you are their grandparents, aunts, uncles. I honor the sacred work you do in these young lives. We must all be alert to these little ones, aware of their needs and attuned to what might be behind their attention-seeking behavior. They need our touch, our smile, our kind discipline, our encouragement, because those ingredients may be missing in the places where they spend most of their time.

When He walked the earth as a man, Jesus said, *"Let the children come to me."* Whenever we are in contact with a child, may God's love within us cause them to be drawn toward Him. We have no way of knowing what the future holds for Chloe and for all the other precious ones in our families, churches and classes, but we know that the Lord has a good plan for each one, and we must do all in our power to help them to desire His plan and to know how precious they are in His sight.

How God Sees Us

My smart little two-and-a-half year old grand-daughter delighted me recently with her rendition of the Gaither song for children which begins, "I am a **P**romise, I am a **P**ossibilility, I am a **P**romise, with a capital **P**." And she is that, as is each child who enters this world, no matter how or where. The words of that song have been going around in my mind as I've watched the Olympics and heard   the stories of some of the athletes who have overcome incredible odds to be able to compete on the world stage. They, their parents and their coaches had to believe in possibility and potentiality.

I don't have to look so far, however, to find examples of people who will never receive publicity for living their lives each day in the belief of what can be. I know grandparents who are rearing their grandchildren. I know a mother whose child has Down Syndrome. I know women who lovingly care for the elderly. I meet young people who are waiting tables while attending college. In our families are single mothers who come home from a day's work to tend to a house and children. In my office each week I sit with couples who believe their relationship can be improved and with singles who believe they can overcome their fears and anxiety. And I believe it, too. I believe in the amazing resilience of the human spirit and in the more amazing power of God to pour His strength into those who seek His help.

At least twice in scripture we're told, *"Nothing is impossible with God."* Hopelessness does not belong in the vocabulary or the thinking of a Christian. We make a big mistake when we dismiss others as outside the realm of God's power to change. He loves everyone of us (and them) as we/they are, but knows what we can be if we let Him control. A question in my Bible study workbook this week was, "What does God see when He looks at you?" I wrote some kind of stock, rather lame answer. I'm going to go back and change it. Just as my granddaughter sings, I believe when God looks at me and at you, He sees, A **P**romise with a capital **P**, **P**ossibility, and a great big bundle of **P**otentiality.

Fifty Years of Blessings

On June 3rd my husband and I will have been married for fifty years. We married six years after we met. We came from similar backgrounds, were both Christians and committed to doing God's will. And we were very much in love. So the great adventure began. I taught school and worked as a hospital dietician. Seven years and two children later, Don finished his medical training, and he and I went on a month-long camping trip. We went from Louisiana to Tennessee to California to Mexico and back to Louisiana, carrying all our equipment in a Volkswagen "bug." We could have sold tickets at every stop for people to watch us repack all that stuff into our little car.

Our next big trip was by boat to Hong Kong, which was to be our home for the next twenty-six years. We had jointly followed God's leading to plant our lives there to share His love with those who did not know Him. Pregnant with our third child, I was seasick every inch of the voyage, while Don blithely ate his way down the ship's extensive menu and described it all to me. We finally arrived, and by the time our daughter was born a few months later, we had already begun our study of the language that no foreigner was ever meant to speak. Every day for three years (during which two more little Langfords joined us) we struggled with the sounds and tones that would help Don to do his medical work and me to buy food in the market. Gradually, we began to feel at home and to love the Chinese people and the bustling international city that never slept. We missed our families and strawberries and pecans, but we knew we were where God meant us to be. We made wonderful friends among the Chinese and our fellow missionaries. We traveled to Taiwan, Japan, Korea, Indonesia, Malaysia, the Philippines, Thailand and China. In Hong Kong, we lived through the Chinese cultural revolution, the Tian An men Square tragedy, and many typhoons. God carried us through the soul-shaking experience of the suicide of our second son. Don was able to give medical help to thousands of patients and I taught the Bible to many women who had never heard God's word before. We helped to build a church which continues to grow. We're grateful for all of our Hong Kong memories and experiences.

Now we're in another season of life. We've cared for each of our parents until the Lord took them home. Don is still working long hours in medicine. I do counseling, write, teach Bible to Chinese graduate students and keep up with our far-flung offspring. Our excellent health is one of God's best gifts. Our life path has not been easy, but never boring. We have disappointed the Lord and each other many times. We've shed many tears, and there's been a lot of laughter. God has graciously given us all these years together, and we are thankful to be able to say that we have kept our commitment to Him and to each other. We look forward to the next adventure He has in store.

Difficulties

Man's Best Friend

Yes, I know the Bradford Pear trees and Japanese magnolias are blooming, and every spring I comment on their beauty, but this time I need to talk about something else. You see, I recently lost a good friend. Her name was Shadow, and I had known her since she was six weeks old. She came to us a friendly, fluffy puppy, in 1996. A pure-bred Australian Shepherd, she won our hearts right away, which made it easier to live through her puppy days of chewing on the wrong things and making puddles in the wrong places. Still, I was not happy when I heard her under the table munching on my glasses. Worst of all was when I found my Bible with deep tooth marks in the leather cover. Apparently, Shadow was especially interested in the book of Matthew.

Our dog grew into an elegant animal with a thick wavy, dark coat accented with white and tan markings. Her greatest joy was just to be with us, whether we were working in the yard, sitting on the patio, or reading at night in the kitchen. She waited to have the last sip of coffee from our cups. She nudged our arms when she wanted to be petted. She lay content at our feet until time for the nightly walk that she and my husband took up the street. She could have spent the rest of her days in those good and simple ways, being fed and cared for by us. But on an evening late in January, Shadow found a gate slightly ajar. She went through it and foolishly wandered into territory where she didn't know how to take care of herself. We found her beautiful broken body in the middle of the road later that night.

I have been surprised at how much I've hurt and how many tears I have shed over Shadow's death. But I've also tried to see if there's anything in the experience that the Lord wants to show to me. Several things are apparent: He has made us for Himself and is most pleased when we are happy to be with Him, expressing and receiving affection, ready to fit into His plans. It is His desire and plan to care for us, and He will do so faithfully if we stay within calling distance. We must not go into unknown territory without Him, our Guide and Protector. He grieves when we make destructive decisions. None of these thoughts are new to you, or to me, but dear Shadow's death reminded me again that these things are true. We are of great value to our loving Father, and we need to stay as close as possible to the hand that feeds us.

Learning Things the Hard Way

$\mathscr{I}$ have spent this summer learning things I didn't want to know. On May 31st I broke my wrist, which then required surgery to install a plate and a pin to hold the pieces in place for healing. About ten days after the operation, I started a three-times-a-week therapy program which still continues. In those early days I had so much pain that I was very protective of my hand and wrist and very fearful of the therapist. They are lovely girls with sweet smiles, but there is no way they can do their job without hurting me. I privately called them my "terror-pists." Gradually as I've gotten to know them better, I've been able to relax somewhat and to trust them more. I can see that the discomfort they cause by bending my unwilling fingers and manipulating my stiff wrist is helping to restore the use of my right hand. I know that my recovery depends on my cooperation with their patient and persistent efforts.

Often when people come to me for counseling, I warn them that the healing they seek may involve some pain. I tell them that they may have to look at things they don't want to see and feel some old hurts they've been covering up. Some folks aren't willing to do this, and so they go away without much change. The ones I love to work with are those who plunge in and who trust me to stand beside them in support as they do what needs to be done in order to bring about healing within themselves or their relationships.

I've learned this summer about broken bones and surgery and the painful process of recovery. I've also learned to do a lot of new things with my left hand. I've seen again how kind and helpful people can be. And I have been reminded again that our loving Father is also one who prunes the fruitful branch, who breaks and remolds the vessel, who chastises His children, sometimes causing pain in order to discipline or restore or cause growth. He molds and bends and stretches us in uncomfortable ways, always urging us toward a more positive and healthy state. As we get to know Him better, the easier it is for us to trust Him. The result He achieved in us depends on that trust, our submission, and our cooperation.

Positive Truths

*A*re you concerned about the downturn in our economy, about job losses, or about bills that might still be unpaid from Christmas? Those are realities, but they are not the only realities. Recently I read about a little girl who was complaining to her mother because they were poor and she did not have many of the things that her friends enjoyed. The mother wisely led her daughter to become aware of riches in ordinary, but often overlooked, places. I've been trying to think more in those terms recently, and have been reminded again of how rich I am:

    – I was born an America, with all the privileges and freedoms that carries.

    – I am in good health, but with good medical care available if I need it.

    – I live in a safe neighborhood where I often walk for exercise as I enjoy golden sunlight and an umbrella of brilliant blue sky.

    – All my children and grandchildren live far away, but I have ready contact with them by phone and e-mail.

    – I have a number of good friends, some of whom I've known for thirty years or more.

    – Every morning a hot cup of coffee is waiting for me when I wake up.

    – Good food is readily available to me in plentiful supply, and I live among the best cooks in the world.

– I have work to do that is helpful to others and fulfilling to me.

– I came to the Lord early in life, and have a secure continuing journey with Him.

I could go on at much more length, but you get the idea. Sometimes I suggest to clients that they carry a little notebook and record the small gifts, the golden moments, in each day. When they do that, they begin to realize that by focusing on the negative realities in their lives, they have missed blessings that are just as real. I invite you to begin to keep a daily account of the riches.

"And I will give thee...hidden riches of secret places, that thou mayest know that I, the Lord, which call thee by thy name, am the god of Israel." Is. 45:3

Open Hearts, Open Homes

$\mathcal{A}$s I write this, we still have Katrina's guests, and we are watching Rita to see whom she will visit. We won't soon forget September, 2005, the month that brought into our cities and homes such tremendous challenges and stress. It has brought frustration and concern as we have watched on our TV screens the ongoing suffering of people fleeing from and trapped in a submerged city. We have also seen and heard wonderful stories of human heroism and of God's grace.

Most of us have become involved in trying to help provide the basic needs of our unexpected guests, whether they were family, friends, or strangers. We have stretched our homes, our pantries, our pocketbooks, and our hearts as we have reached out to them with southern hospitality seasoned with big doses of Christian love. We may have even surprised ourselves with our willingness to share what we have and to find more when it is needed. We are thankful to be in a position to help others and to experience the blessing of being able to give. During these days our pastors have been examples of compassion and service, and our churches have opened their gyms, kitchens, family life centers, and other facilities. We have done what was right and what was needed. So many of you have gone above and beyond the call of duty as you have served the displaced folks among us.

At our house, we've "adopted" two delightful young couples, neither of whom we knew before Katrina introduced us. One couple is Chinese, but speaks a different dialect from the one we know. The other is a vegetarian, who came with a cat named Ruth and a yellow Labrador dog, both of which were used to being indoors. Need I say that adjustments have been made on a daily basis by all concerned?

We do not know how long our help will be needed, so we need to think in terms of pacing ourselves physically. We need to be patient with ourselves as well as those in our homes and shelters. Most importantly, we must draw aside daily to center ourselves in the One who has given us enough to share and who wants to use us to help further His good plan for every disarranged life. Keep up the good work!

Those Left Behind

*T*his week I attended a meeting of survivors. Everyone present had lost a loved one to suicide. For one couple, it was a beautiful young daughter, for another, a teenage son. A young husband had lost his wife. One dear lady's son had taken his life, and only months later, her daughter died in a car wreck. I sat among them and shared their pain. They meet twice a month to support each other as they deal with their losses.

Actually, survivors are all around us. We all know those who have battled cancer with every method at their disposal. Our friends and family members have lived through terrible accidents and injuries. Fellow church members and co-workers have had strokes, heart attacks, brain tumors, and have suffered abuse of all sorts. Some of them see themselves as victims, but most of them get past that mind-set and think of themselves as survivors. And some go on to learn all they can from the unwanted experience, using it to enrich their own lives and to benefit others. They exemplify Romans 8:37 – *"Know in all these things we are more than conquerors through Him who loved us."* I never cease to be amazed at what the human spirit can endure and rise above, especially when that spirit is linked to the all-powerful Spirit of God.

One of the reasons I became a counselor was to try to help other families avoid the kind of incredible pain that we felt when our second son took his own life in 1984. The path through that pain was slow and arduous, but the Lord was with us for every step of it. Each year since that time, my husband and I try to do something to mark our son's life in a positive way. This year we are preparing to participate in the first annual walk to raise funds for the Foundation of Suicide Prevention. Along with about 3000 other people, we will start at sunset and walk through the night, 26 miles into Washington, D.C. My head tells me I can do it. Now I'm trying to get my body ready. I want to join with those I know who, with God's help, keep going and overcome, refusing to be victims or even survivors, but to be victorious in those experiences that would crush us without His power. *"Thanks be to God! He gives us the victory through our Lord Jesus Christ!"* I Cor. 15:57

Waiting on God

At our house we are learning our own version of walking by faith and not by sight. Two weeks ago my husband had surgery to close a hole that had appeared in the macula of his "good" eye. (Vision in the other eye is greatly affected by a cataract.) We approached the operation as we do all life events: trusting God to be in control and to bring about the best possible results. After surgery, Don carefully followed the doctor's instruction to lie face down for five days. We thought the recovery of his sight would take only a matter of a few more days. Now we have learned that it could take as long as six months. We're still adjusting to this surprising news. But we also know it was no surprise to the Lord, and we're still trusting Him and trying to learn the lessons that need to come from this experience.

We always want things to happen quickly, don't we? Even when we pray for patience, we want it right now! We and our children have grown used to "quick this" and "instant that". We expect to push a button and get a product. But some of life's most important results are those which can only occur over time. A phrase I often use in the counseling office is: "Time is your friend." In time, difficult teenagers grow into responsible young people, marriage partners forgive each other of wounds to their relationship, grieving families learn how to carry the memory of their loved one as they move on with life, those who've gone through divorce pick up the pieces and make a new beginning. But all these things happen by a process, often one that is slow and painful, and one in which it is sometimes hard to keep trusting that God is at work for good in our lives.

The day before the doctor delivered our disappointing news, our pastor ended his sermon with this quote from Andrew Murray, who surely understood about time and process and God's purpose: "Say, He brought me here. It is by His will I am in this strait place, and in that fact I will rest. He will keep me here in His love and give me grace to behave as His child. Then He will make the trial a blessing, teaching me the lessons He intends for me to learn. In His good time, He can bring me out again – how and when He knows." Don and I are trusting that God.

Beyond These Circumstances

$\mathscr{I}$ write this on a cold, gray, damp day. The news is not good. Oil prices are plummeting. (Good for our gas tanks, but not for our economy.) California's citrus crop has been decimated by cold weather. Closer to home, workers have been laid off from the salt mine because unseasonably warm weather in the north meant they didn't need salt for their roads. Already this year, we've had a record number of deaths by auto accidents, fires and homicides in our area. In my work as a counselor, I hear story after story of loss, anxiety, betrayal. Personally, my heart is burdened for one relative and three dear friends who are literally in a life or death battle with illness, not to mention the other needs on my prayer list.

All of the above is true. But it is not the only truth. When God walked the earth in human form, He told us that in this world we would have tribulation. Then He quickly urged us not to be afraid, because He has overcome the world. And He promises that He will never leave us or forsake us. As often as is appropriate, I try to remind my counseling clients of what He gives to those of us who belong to Him. In the first chapter of Ephesians I read that this world is not the only reality. There is another realm, just as real, and even more vital. In that realm we are surrounded by His love, which means that everything that comes to us has been filtered through that love. That passage goes on to declare that we are blessed, chosen, adopted, (it gets even better) accepted, redeemed and forgiven. So no matter what else is going on, we must look for and thank Him for each day's blessings. We can revel in the fact that He wanted each of us. He draws us to Himself, and then actually calls us His children. In Him, if nowhere else, we are accepted just as we are. He formed each one of us according to His plan and for His purpose and pleasure. But we've all messed up the plan at some point. That's when our loving Father reaches down, lifts us up, hears our repentance, and declares us to be forgiven and redeemed, clean in His sight. In the midst of bad weather, disturbing news, serious illness, irreplaceable losses, we have a Rock, a Hiding Place, where there is love, blessing, acceptance, redemption, forgiveness – and more. Trust this for yourself and share it with others.

Why Are We Still Here?

$\mathcal{T}$hese recent weeks have been full of storms. First came the horrific cyclone in the poor country of Myanmar, where the death toll is expected to surpass 125,000. Then followed the terrifying earthquake in China, with the number of dead now past 80,000 and rising. Our own community and surrounding areas felt the results of a powerful tornado whose winds randomly swept through business and residential areas, breaking trees in half, pushing out windows and damaging roofs. One interesting question to ask ourselves is which of these events concerned us the most.

Here in south Louisiana, we know how to deal with the consequences of Mother Nature's whims. We're old hands at going days without electricity and at repairing wind and water damage. One of our recent newspapers quoted this year's high school graduates in our city speaking of the traumas and storms that they have known during their school years: 9/11, Katrina, Rita, the deaths of classmates. They spoke with surprising maturity of how they have faced these events as a family, drawn strength from each other, and learned the value of community. Young as they are, some of them have learned that there can be value in adversity.

Tomorrow I will be speaking to the group of Chinese

graduate students with whom I meet every Sunday morning. What can I say to them about the tragedy in their country and about this sort of thing which has happened throughout history? First, I will have to say that I don't know why these natural events occur, and I don't think anyone else does, either. I will say that we need to use our mental, emotional, physical and financial resources to do all we can to help the survivors in any way we can. And I will refer them to Luke 13:1-5 where Jesus makes it clear that trauma and tragedy should cause us to examine our own lives to be sure that every day is spent in ways that are pleasing to the Lord and useful in His kingdom. How many days do we have left before the next storm and where will it hit? We can't know that, but we are His; our lives are in His hands, and someone's eternity may depend on our witness.

Man's Anger

"To dwell above with those we love, that will be such glory! But to live below with those we know, well, that's another story!" I smiled when I heard those lines on the radio recently, but it set me to thinking about so many of the people I see in counseling who are angry with those who are closest to them – husbands and wives, parents and children, brothers and sisters, other family members, friends. I deal with a lot of angry people, and most of them want to be rid of their negative feelings. It may surprise you to know that I don't encourage that in every case. That's because some anger is appropriate. I believe that is so when a child has been abused in any way, and in a few other specific situations. In those cases, anger serves as the energy to rescue the one being mistreated, stand up to the perpetrator, and ideally, bring that person to justice.

Most of the time, however, I agree that even though the anger a person feels may be justified, it is better to find a healthy way to express it. I usually point out that the rush of adrenalin we identify as anger probably originates in fear, hurt or frustration. Then I try to guide folks to label which of those they need to deal with. The Bible instructs us to *"be angry and sin not,"* which I understand to mean that anger itself is not a sin. It's what we do or say when "mad" that can be very destructive. So in the counseling office we do a lot of talking about ways to express negative feelings without harming people or property. We talk about ways to lovingly confront, and encourage safe, open communication, so "explosions" won't be so likely to occur. We also talk about teaching children what they can do when they are angry, because most of us were only taught what we should not do. And I encourage my clients to learn to respond rather than react, taking time to choose the best word or action. As long as we live below with those we know, we will sometimes have negative feelings toward them. James 1:19-20 has been very helpful to me at such times: *"My dear brothers, take note of this: Everyone should be quick to listen, slow to speak and slow to become angry, for man's anger does not achieve God's purpose."*

Learning to Number Our Days

As I write this I am keenly aware of the fragility of life. There are several reasons for this awareness. One reason is my age. I have come to the place in life when my friends are beginning to have serious illnesses or to pass from this earth. In recent weeks I have received word from three of our former fellow missionaries in Hong Kong that they are now battling life-threatening diseases. Tomorrow I am to spend time with a friend from California who has been receiving intensive treatment for cancer. A friend called this week from West Texas to ask for prayer because of the very unwelcome diagnosis she has received.

In very recent weeks in the counseling office I have met with those who are dealing with the aftermath of the loss of a loved one. And I have spoken with one who has been told that death will come before the year ends.

I am not a gloomy person, but can you understand why I feel that I am walking through a mine field? Here are some things I am learning from these who are facing the last great enemy:

1. We need to thank our Creator/Sustainer each day for the gift of life.
2. Christians are not immune to disease or to accidents.

3. When these unwanted guests enter our lives, He is bigger then they are. He walks with us. He really is able to give peace and comfort, strength and courage to those who are ill and to those who love them.

4. When our family members, friends, fellow church members are very ill and have suffered a loss, we must walk with them in whatever way we can. Our own fear, discomfort, or lack of knowledge is beside the point. We serve Him by giving support through notes, phone calls, food, flowers, prayer, and sometimes just by our presence. We must help them to know they are surrounded by His love which flows through us as fellow pilgrims.

5. Someday it will be our turn. Let us stay ready. Confess sin. Forgive offenses. Play with children or grandchildren. Tell people you love them. Trust the lord in every area of life and encourage others to do the same.

6. Trust His promises concerning what we cannot know. He said that we are unable to imagine the things that He has prepared for those who love Him. Only our ignorance causes us to cling so tenaciously to our earthly lives. This world is not our permanent home.

Special Days

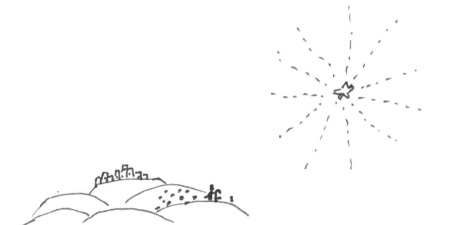

Lessons Learned in Hong Kong

Tomorrow will be Chinese New Year and the fortieth anniversary of the day that my husband, two little boys and I arrived in Hong Kong to begin our missionary adventure there. My mind has been flooded with memories this week as I thought of those days and of the years that followed and all that we experienced in that unique place. I could fill a book with all I learned during our time in Asia, but today I share just four lessons:

1) We have much to learn from those who are different from ourselves. I went to Hong Kong full of American pride. Fairly soon, however, I began to see that the Chinese people have customs that are worth emulating. They honor and revere the elderly. They are extremely gracious and hospitable people, always offering a guest the best they have, even if it means denying themselves. Sometimes they even accompany their guest all the way home to be sure he arrives safely! If they are the visitor, they always bring a gift, no matter how humble. And they are survivors. Through 5000 plus years of history, they have learned to bend in the storm like bamboo, but not break.

2) A person can bring dignity to any kind of work. I remember the tall shoe-repair man who would sit on a small stool at our front door, doing leather work with simple tools and patiently teaching Chinese phrases to

our children. And all my friends in the street market who sold vegetables, fruit and meat from their primitive stalls, cheerful no matter what the weather. I think of a carpenter friend who spoke no English, but always understood better than we how to design and build what we needed.

3) This one is just for fun: There is almost nothing you can do with one chopstick, but many things can be done with two. For me, this is a symbol for cooperation and of how we all need each other in so many ways.

4) Lastly, I saw over and over that God's Word is alive. Through all those years, as I met with people who had never read the Bible or known its message, I watched as the Holy Spirit stirred their hearts and minds, caused them to ask questions, interpreted its meaning in terms they could understand, and drew them to Himself. This is why I cannot counsel others without using God's Word. And it is why I am thankful for all of you who live each day to share His Word with others.

I say to you all, "KUNG HEY FAHT CHOY", Happy New Year!

A Tribute to Mothers

We <u>must</u> talk about mothers in May. Certainly it is appropriate at my house, for the month contains both Mother's Day and my mother's birthday. On the fourth of the month Mother will be ninety-four years old. It will be like any other day to her, because she long ago lost track of day and dates. We will celebrate though, and probably with something chocolate, because I know she likes that, although she can no longer tell me so. We will have candles, and we will sing while she looks placidly from face to face. We'll hold hands and pray, thanking God for her life and for her many years of service to His church and to our family by her cooking, sewing, visiting, giving and singing. She won't remember, but we will.

On Mother's Day I'll be thinking of her again, and of our daughter, who recently became a mother for the third time. She does her job well, caring for three little boys with strength, love and humor. Like so many other mothers, she is teacher, protector, comforter, provider, disciplinarian and more. She is aware that the effect she has on her sons each day will affect other lives for years to come.

I meet with a variety of mothers who come to the counseling office. Some are sad because they are estranged from a child. Others are seeking help in dealing with children who are rebellious. Some are in grief because they have lost a child to death. Still others want to know how to help a little one who is struggling in school and those who have been abused. Though each story is different, they all have one great attribute in common: every mother loves her children regardless of what they have done or the pain they may have caused. A mother cannot not love.

And here's the amazing thing: There is a love even greater than a mother's love. The psalmist said, *"When my mother and father forsake me, then will the Lord take care of me."* (Psalm 27:10, NKJV)

A Change in Plans

The saying, "If you want to make God laugh, tell Him your plans" surely applies to the day I've had today. My plan was to get to my computer first thing this morning and write a lovely piece that would turn hearts and minds toward Thanksgiving, causing all who read it to be more aware of their many blessings. Well, that didn't happen, but a lot of other things did. Before I had finished breakfast, plumbers arrived at my door, tools in hand, ready to install a new kitchen faucet and do other minor repairs which I needed to point out to them. After they left, my mother's care-giver heard a mysterious dripping inside a wall, so I became a drip detective, checking outside pumps and attic drip pans, looking for the source of the sound, fearing the worst.

Then I had to make a trip to the bank to straighten out an error in our account, followed by a foray to the drug store to stock up on supplies needed by my mother. Back home just in time to take her to the eye doctor. Not simple, this involves loading and unloading a wheelchair and lifting Mother into and out of it. After the appointment, I went to get the eye drops which the doctor had prescribed. "Sixty-six dollars!" I exclaimed when I got back into the car. And my mother who goes days without speaking at all said, "Sixty-six dollars!" We returned home just in time for me to start cooking supper.

So, what does all this have to do with Thanksgiving? Well, in my counseling training I learned about reframing, looking at a situation from a different perspective. Or you may think of it as using the lemons of life to make lemonade. So here goes: I'm thankful for plumbers, even if they arrive in the middle of breakfast. I'm thankful that my husband seems to have located the source of the leak. I'm thankful that the bank error was corrected and in my favor! I'm thankful for doctors who can diagnose what's wrong and for medication when we need it. I'm thankful that about once a week Mother let's us know that she's still in there. And I'm thankful for a simple supper with family after a day orchestrated not by me, but by the Lord. I encourage you to play the Reframe Game often. Happy Thanksgiving!

A Father's Gift

Remember my writing class? Recently the assignment was for us to write about an influential person in our lives. I wrote about my dad. He was a patient and godly man who had a great sense of humor, a positive outlook, and a heart for people. He taught me many good things by word and example. Due to his influence I learned to pray about decisions and to seek God's will for my life. Most of all, he loved me, no matter how foolish or immature, thoughtless or disobedient I was. He gave me the immeasurable gift of self-worth.

As I sit in the counseling office, I often hear stories of fathers who are/were very different from my dad. The sinful choices they have made have laid burdens on their children that they need human and divine help to deal with. As I work with those "children," I try to help them come to understand that God is the loving, perfect Father they did not have on earth. I try to present Him as the ultimate Promise Keeper, a trustworthy Guide, an unfailing Source of wisdom and strength.

December is the month when we celebrate the time when that Almighty Father chose to take a human form and enter history as a baby. He did so in order to show us what He is like and to express His love by giving Himself in payment for all sin: the sin of the fathers, the mothers, and the children. May your Christmas celebration and mine center around His gift of love.

The Value of Truth

𝔅esides Valentine's Day, the month of February contains the birthdays of two presidents, both known for positive aspects of character. When questioned about a childhood misdeed, George Washington reportedly answered, "I cannot tell a lie." Then there was Abraham Lincoln, called "Honest Abe" because of many examples of the value he placed on truthfulness and reliability. These men are described in history books as personifications of integrity. Their words matched their deeds.

In recent days television reports and newspapers are full of stories about the current president. All of us are wondering whether or not he is telling the truth. Is he a man of integrity; do his actions match his words?

In the counseling office I see people who are unhappy because they have been untrue to what they know to be right. Or perhaps they have been betrayed by someone they trusted. Maybe they are suffering the consequences of having deceived themselves or someone else. Part of my job is to help them to face facts, to accept reality, to see the truth and then to cope with it, make restitution, or take other appropriate action.

There can be no doubt in our minds as to how much God values honesty. Jesus calls himself the Truth. He commended the Samaritan woman for her truthfulness. And He directed his followers to let their "yea be yea" and their "nay be nay." For the sake of our own mental, emotional and spiritual health and for the sake of those who watch our lives, let us determine to be people whose actions and words are the same, examples of integrity, people who speak and live the truth.

He Is Risen Indeed!

*A*lmost everyone who makes an appointment with me has a problem. Every day that I sit in my office, I listen to stories of difficulty, disagreements and loss. And each time I drive to the office, I pray that God will give me His wisdom, His insight, His words to help those who come, and that He will help me to point them to Him for their answers.

At home I receive letters, e-mails and phone calls informing me of special needs of friends and family members: serious illnesses, marriage problems, difficulties with children, deaths. I pray for these loved ones and send messages reminding them of our loving Father's promises. What would we do if we did not have a living Lord? Where would we turn? Paul said it well in Cor. 15:14: *"If Christ has not been raised, our preaching is useless and so is your faith." A dead God could not walk with us through the trials of this life. But our God lives!*

In Westminster Abbey I have walked among the graves of some of the great leaders of history. Their bones are there or have returned to dust. In Paris I stood at the massive marble stone marking the burial place of Napoleon, unmoved since he was placed beneath it. In China I stood in line to file past the body of

Mao Tse Tung. He lies under glass, one of death's trophies. In Xian I walked to the top of the burial mound of China's first emperor, the builder of the Great Wall. He lies where he has been since 210 B.C. I have seen the eternal flame that burns at the Arlington Cemetery grave of J.F. Kennedy. I have read the inscription on Benjamin Franklin's headstone. I have been to the Protestant Cemetery in Macau to view the grave of Robert Morrison who first translated the scriptures into Chinese. But I have only been to one resurrection site. On a bright, clear day I visited the simple garden near a skull-shaped hill just outside Jerusalem. I saw the groove in front of the cave-like burial place which had held a great stone to cover the entrance. I read the simple sign over the low doorway: "He is not here, for He is risen!" I entered the tomb itself. It is silent. And it is empty.

Our own faith and what we have to offer to others is based on those eight wonderful words. Our Lord is the One who has overcome the world and its last enemy. Happy Easter!

Living Life God's Way

I write this just before Thanksgiving, and when you read it, we will all be looking toward Christmas and a new year. It's that annual time when we look back and count our blessings, take stock of lessons learned, and make resolutions about our behavior in days to come. Like many of you, I am in a church that is working its way through Rick Warren's excellent book, The Purpose Driven Life. Today's reading focused on having balance in one's life. In that chapter Warren quotes from Lam. 3:40 in The Message: *"Let's take a good look at the way we're living and reorder our lives under God."* A perfect verse for where we are in our year.

So let's think a bit about balance. I don't think that means that every area of our lives should have equal time, but it does mean that one activity or area of responsibility doesn't take so much of our time and energy that there is little left for other areas of concern. Following the urging of Jeremiah, let's take a good look at the way we are living. Isn't it true that one of the statements we make most often is, "I don't have enough time?" But wasn't it God himself who decided how long each day would be? One of my favorite writers, Elizabeth Elliot says it well, "There will be time enough in every day, you can count on it, to do everything that God intends you to do."

It's that last phrase that's the key—what God intends. We're reminded in <u>The Purpose Driven Life</u> that our life on earth is preparation for eternity. So it follows, doesn't it, that we need to give time and effort emphasis to those things that have eternal value, and we need to be leading our families and encouraging others to do the same. But we are human beings with some basic needs, so we need to take care of ourselves physically and emotionally. And since this life and the next centers around relationship, we must give priority to time with the Lord and with those He's given to us.

My counsel to my clients (and to myself) is that every week should include work, food for the spirit, self-care, time with family/friends, service to others, learning, creativity, and something for personal enjoyment. You're welcome to revise that list as you see fit, but let's take a good look at the way we're living our lives and reorder our lives under God. May our Christmas and the New Year be all that He intends.

God with Us! Celebrate!

This title recently caught my eye in a Christian publication: "The Top 10 Reasons Why I Don't Celebrate Christmas." The writer of the article listed and expounded on his reasons for "kicking the Christmas habit." As I scanned his piece, I had to admit that some of what he put forward was quite valid. He said Christmas is driven by commercialism, that it is nowhere to be found in the Bible, that Jesus wasn't born on or near December 25th. He further stated that Christmas is largely a recycled pagan celebration, that God condemns using pagan customs to worship Him, and that you can't put Christ back into something He was never in. He also claims that Christmas obscures God's plan for mankind. I read the article with interest, trying to keep an open mind. But the writer didn't win me over to his anti–Christmas position.

I will continue to celebrate this special season, and here are more than ten of my reasons: <u>The Sounds of Christmas</u>: laughter as friends and family come together, shouts of children happy to have a holiday, phone calls just to say "I love you;" and the music, filling our ears and our hearts with the wonderful old songs and surprising new compositions that express as nothing else can the wonder of God come to earth in human form. <u>The Smells of Christmas</u>: turkey roasting, pies baking, fresh pine boughs on the mantel, fragrant candles, cookies warm from the oven, all ways of celebrating the material abundance God has chosen to give us along with His Son. <u>The Sights of Christmas</u> – colorful and creative decorations in shops, offices, and homes, gorgeous red poinsettias massed in front of the church; flickering candlelight, smiles on faces of people who know a secret. <u>The Feelings of Christmas</u>: being with those who are dear to us, remembering those who are no longer with us, enjoying a baby's first Christmas, worshiping with other believers. And every year, some kind of defining <u>Moment of Christmas</u>: giving or receiving the perfect, unexpected gift, sharing with or serving someone who cannot reciprocate, seeing a person come to understand the meaning of the celebration, watching or being part of a long-sought reconciliation.

I know that Jesus wasn't born on December 25th. But He <u>was</u> born, choosing to become one of us, in order to show us the Father and how life was meant to be lived. Without His birth, there would be no death or resurrection. I will celebrate that miracle in every way I can. And I will pray that the celebration will continue throughout the new year in each of our lives. Emmanuel!

The Power of Easter

There is no holiday more special than Easter, and I have spent this special day in many wonderful ways. Thinking back over the years, I have a wealth of Easter memories. In my childhood, my mother would make a pretty new pastel dress and take me to buy shiny new patent leather shoes. It was on the night before Easter in my seventeenth year that a person who is still very special to me first said, "I love you." On Easter morning he sent a single fragrant gardenia for me to wear on my new navy linen Mother-made suit.

Each year at Easter I pull up the memory of a picture of our first two sons, ages one and four years, so innocent and sweet with their baskets, bunnies and Easter suits. I recall hiding eggs for the children to find among the bamboo, bougainvillea, firecracker vines and papaya trees in our yard in Hong Kong. When the children were older, we spent one Easter holiday with a church group on board a somewhat refurbished Chinese junk, sailing the South China Sea, sleeping on deck under the stars.

An especially glorious Easter was spent with my sister at the height of tulip time in the Netherlands – indescribable beauty! But my very favorite Easter memory is of the one my husband and I spent at the garden tomb outside Jerusalem's city wall. We actually walked into the hillside cave, saw its mottled gray walls and the stone table where the body would have been placed. The tomb was cool, silent and empty, just the way the disciples found it that first Easter.

Wherever you spend Easter this year, may you be greeted with the declaration, "He is risen!" and may you reply with joy, "He is risen indeed!" And on every day may you be encouraged by the words of Eph. 1:19-20a: *"How very great is His power at work in us who believe...the same as the mighty strength which He used when he raised Christ from death..."*

If My People

We all very much aware of the spiritual needs of our nation. From the nation's highest office and across the breadth of our country, we have daily evidence of the results of man's sinful choices. In the counseling office I deal with these consequences as they affect marriages, families, and individual lives. In His word the Lord gives direction to His people which will lead to blessing for a nation. As we approach Thanksgiving, a national holiday, may I share with you a prayer written in response to Chronicles 7:14.

IF MY PEOPLE, WHICH ARE CALLED BY MY NAME SHALL HUMBLE THEMSELVES...

Lord, I don't think I can humble myself. When I try, I compare myself to others, and I become proud of my humility. But I am willing to be made humble. Will you do it, Lord, starting now? Make me aware of presumptuous sins. Use whatever means You will to teach me to be humble.

AND PRAY...

Are you sad, Father, that we plan so much and work so hard, yet pray so little? Teach us to delight in Your presence, to seek Your face, to praise, to intercede, to wait for You to lead.

AND TURN FROM THEIR WICKED WAYS...

Lord, I am so aware, so alert, so perceptive concerning the sins of others. Show me my own wickedness. Help me to see myself as You see me. Uncover the wrongs I have buried or called by some sweet name. Dress them in their true colors and parade them before me. Help me to confess them gladly and not look back.

Give me, I pray, the will and the strength to fulfill the conditions of "IF MY PEOPLE" and then to trust You to perform all the promises of "THEN WILL I..."

No Greater Gift

The year is winding down, stores are displaying must-have merchandise, holiday outfits and the latest toys. Soon Christmas carols will fill the air and poinsettias will be celebrating in scarlet. The old story will be depicted in music, in plays and in silent nativity scenes. Each one will feature a manger holding the Christ child, the one who came to bring so many life-changing gifts, and none more valuable than forgiveness.

Each week I am reminded of how important it is to forgive and be forgiven. Why is it so difficult to do? Forgiving doesn't mean saying the hurt or offense didn't happen or didn't matter. Nor does it mean forgetting. Some awful wounds cannot be forgotten. But we can learn to remember them in a new way. It is possible to choose to let them go, picture them being handed to God for Him to deal with, along with the one who committed the wrong. Forgiveness doesn't mean I don't have a right to be angry or to "get even." It means that I picture myself standing with my offender at the foot of the cross, acknowledging that we both are guilty of sins for which the Christmas Child suffered and died. It means that I listen in amazement and learn from the One who never sinned, as He prays for the very ones who put Him to death, *"Father, forgive them, for they know not what they do."*

Is there someone you need to forgive, or someone of whom you need to ask forgiveness? Do it now, so you can sing the carols with a light heart, so you can enter the New Year with a clean slate. Do it now, to bring healing and blessing. Honor Him by using the gift He brought with His birth, the gift He taught by His death.

Deo Volente

I'm writing this in November, looking ahead to this month's holiday and to the ones that follow. Seven adult family members and our two precious granddaughters will be with us for Thanksgiving, so I'm already planning what I want to serve them to eat for each day of their visit. Then my husband and I will go to Dallas for his birthday and Christmas and on to Chicago to spend New Year's and my birthday with family there. I'm already looking into travel plans for an overseas mission trip we're to make in late January. Lots of exciting stuff and happy times coming up!

In my quiet moments, I can't help wondering if God is shaking His head and laughing, because He knows what's <u>really</u> going to happen. Recently I've been going through the book of James with my Chinese Sunday School class. You will recall that James warns us regarding boasting about what we will do tomorrow and the next day, as if we had control over future events. The Puritans apparently had a good understanding of what James wanted to convey. They ended their letters with the words "Deo Volente," Latin for "if God wills." John Wesley and the early Methodists also adopted this practice. I suppose it was the more somber version of what we used to hear our grandparents say: "I'll do thus and so, the good Lord willin' and the creek don't rise."

Were those earlier folks more aware of something we may have forgotten? Of course, we must make plans, buy groceries before guests arrive and buy airline tickets, but I think James was talking about an attitude of the heart. Have you ever made plans and then asked the Lord to bless them? Do we ever try to carry out our own designs, and then call on God to get us out of the mess we've made? On my best days I recall what Henry Blackaby said: that we need to find out what God is doing and join Him there, not get on our horse and ride off in all directions.

Maybe it's the fact that another birthday is rolling quickly toward me, or maybe it's because in these recent months I have experienced the deaths of several friends and a dear family member, but whatever the reason, I don't want to waste any of the time I have left. I'm always full of my own ideas, but I want to fit in with God's plan. So as this year winds down and a new one begins, I find myself in company with James, the Puritans, John Wesley and my grandparents. I want to have a keen awareness every day that it is God who is sovereign over the events in our lives. I want to approach each day in humble submission to His divine plan. I want to remember Proverbs 19:21: *"Many are the plans in a man's heart, but it is the Lord's purpose that prevails."*

The Gift of Self

You've started thinking about Christmas gifts, haven't you? And so have I. Although I complain that the stores display trees, wreaths and other decorations along with the Halloween merchandise, their ploy works, and at some level of my brain, I start thinking about whom to buy for and what to buy. None of our children live near, so we're at the gift certificate stage with them. The grandchildren are far away too, so I need a lot of help to know who is the action hero du jour or what is the latest Game Boy fad. Besides, I really want to give my family and friends gifts that have meaning. My greatest wish is to find ways to share time and myself with them.

I think of them more and more as I sit in my office and listen to wives who long for time with their husbands who work all week and then play golf, hunt or watch TV all weekend. Then there are the husbands who feel they've been forgotten because their wives are involved in a career or with the children or other activities. Recently I have heard several young women say they didn't really know their dads. Another told me she often asked her mom to spend time with her, but the mother was "too busy."

I'm sure you don't want any of the above to apply to you and yours. This Christmas let's be creative and purposeful with our gifts. If I give my grandson a book, I think I'll put a note in saying I want to read it with him. Or I can try to find something we could do together for someone less fortunate. Maybe the gift certificates I send could be for a weekend trip together or for time together on a special project. I could make coupons for a long, newsy telephone call each week or for a time to visit my daughters and take care of all their mending or make casseroles for the freezer. My husband is easy; I could just rent old John Wayne or Jimmy Stewart Westerns to watch with him now and then. I'm just brain-storming here and inviting you to do so. Let's give fewer things and more of ourselves this year, taking as our example the One who is the reason for Christmas – Emmanuel – God With Us.

Stones of Remembrance

$\mathcal{B}$ack in the 70's when the American military was leaving Vietnam, missionaries were told to pack one bag each and leave quickly. When the suitcase of one little boy was unpacked, it was found to contain only the family rock collection. At first, his parents were very unhappy that he hadn't packed clothes, but the more they thought about it, they realized he had chosen to bring something very valuable and irreplaceable – a sort of family history represented by rocks from places they had been together. I can relate to that little fellow, as I have a more modest collection, but one that is important to me. I have a rock I picked up on the shore of the Sea of Galilee, another from beside the frigid North Sea. I acquired a stone recently on part of the Ring of Kerry in Ireland, and I have one I picked up the day my 90-year-old mother and I revisited my birthplace.

Recently I've been reading again those Old Testament stories which emphasize the importance of stones of remembrance. Remember when Joshua led the Israelites to cross over the Jordan into the Promised Land, with the priests standing mid-stream until all had passed through? Then God instructed Joshua to set up a memorial of twelve stones as a reminder of what had happened in the place on that day. He wanted the people to have a visual reminder which would prompt questions from their descendents, so they could tell their children of the power and faithfulness of the God they served.

As we approach this Thanksgiving season, we might consider using stones of remembrance with our own families. Special experiences of God's help and care could be written on real or paper stones. The collection could be added to all through the year and could be read through every Thanksgiving. Children (and the rest of us) need concrete objects to see and touch to help them understand a concept. Even if we live alone or have no children in the household, we all have many reasons to start a collection of stones of remembrance of God's personal care of each of us. I'd love to hear about your rock collection. Happy Thanksgiving!

Thoughts for the New Year

𝒜 year is ending. Another will begin soon. This is the time when we look back in review of the events, experiences, mistakes and blessings of the past twelve months. Although everything that has happened has not been positive, I come to this year's end remembering many good gifts from the hand of my Heavenly Father. I've had thousands of miles of safe travel, I've experienced cultures other than my own. I've participated in times of special celebration with family and friends. I've had good health and met some physical challenges. I've been able to share with others what the Lord has given to me in terms of money, housing, training and experience. And through it all, I've been aware of His living, loving presence.

I look forward to a fresh new year and to the adventures and lessons it will hold. As I enter its threshold, I offer myself anew to Him, and I believe that will be achieved at least partly as I live a life of balance. As we look together toward a new beginning, may I share with you an outline I sometimes offer to people in the counseling office when they are needing to move forward to a more meaningful life. I suggest to them that in every week they include some activity that will promote spiritual growth, another that will be good for physical health, work that is done to the best of their ability, some act that will benefit or be a service to others, a social time with friends and/or family, some time of quiet and solitude, a time of learning something new, and some kind of creative activity. Does that sound like a good formula to you? If so, join me in using it as a guide in the new year.

As the days, weeks, and months come and go, whatever the number of the year, I want to be true to the One who has never failed me. As I have done for so many years, once again I say to Him, "I would be your servant. For this I was created: Before my birth you called my name to do Your will, to be Your light, to bring salvation, to use Your strength, to give You glory. Humbly, gladly, always, I would be Your servant."

My Computer

Insecure Server

Lately little messages are popping up on my computer that I don't like to see. I depend on my old Compaq to receive and send messages, to find info on the Internet, and to be available when I need to do a bit of writing. Now it's saying things to me like, "the server you are using has a certificate that is not secure" and even worse, "the server has failed." A technician assures me that there is a way to fix the problem, and I'm sure we'll find it in due time, but the bottom line is that I cannot always depend on the machine. My computer sometimes disappoints me.

People sometimes disappoint us too, don't they? They make promises they don't keep. They can't or won't give us what we'd like to have from them emotionally. They don't always tell the truth. They're unavailable when we need them. These are the kinds of complaints I often hear in the counseling office. I try to help people see that, since we can't control the behavior of others, probably we need to adjust our own expectations, which I realize is easier said than done.

How grateful I am that I have never had to adjust my expectations of my Heavenly Father. He promises never to leave me or forsake me. He says His eyes are upon us from the beginning to the end of the year. He promises to be our Comforter when needed. He says He will pity us as a father pities his children. And He declares that when we face life's difficulties and trials, we can be more than conquerors through Him. Those words and the truth of them have endured through the ages. No chance of an "insecure certificate" or a "server that fails." He is the eternal Promise Keeper. And we belong to Him.

How Old Are You?

$\mathcal{D}$o you know your Real Age? I'm sure you know if you are 36 or 63, but what is your body's age in terms of health? Some time ago I was introduced to a web site on the Internet call RealAge.com. There I found a rather lengthy quiz about my dietary and exercise habits and my general lifestyle. When I completed the quiz, the computer presented me with its conclusion as to my Real Age, which I'm happy to tell you was nine years younger than my actual age , which I'm not telling you.

That experience has set me to thinking how interesting it would be if there were a similar test we could take which would reveal our ages in terms of our dealings with each other. Such a test would calibrate our responses to loss, disappointment, or to getting our own way. It would show whether we just react emotionally to life situations or take time to think and to choose a good response.

Every week I spend hours observing and dealing with people of varying emotional ages and levels of spiritual maturity. I sit with them in the consequences brought on by someone who expresses anger like a two-year-old or by one who pouts like a child when she can't have something she wants. I see adults who view life as being too hard, like a math problem they can't solve.

I see the havoc wrought by a partner who childishly sought instant gratification in destructive ways. Then on Sunday I listened amazed as a 12-year-old Chinese girl told that, while on a recent trip, she realized that spiritual development is more important than education. What is that child's real age?

I invite you to check out the RealAge web site, just for fun. And I remind all of us that God has given us some very specific measures in His word for gauging our spiritual maturity and for guiding our growth into the image of His Son. See His web sites at Matthew 5-7 and Ephesians 4-6.

Redoing History

Almost every time I sit down at my computer I learn something new about it. Recently I discovered a wonderful command. If I click on "Edit," one possibility listed there is this one: Undo/Redo History. You can be sure that I have used it a lot since I found it. I so often make mistakes on the computer, hitting the wrong key and setting in motion an action that is not at all what I want to happen. I have found, to my delight, that clicking on "Undo/Redo History" will immediately put things back like they were.

Not only have I found the command to be of practical use at the computer, but I have continued to think about it in another context. Wouldn't it be wonderful if we had an "Edit" menu available somewhere in our lives? We could just click on it and undo that irritable attitude we had toward a family member or the argument we had with a friend. We could redo the unwise choices that put us into bad situations. We could erase the wrong decisions. We could put broken relationships back like they were. If only we could undo/redo history!

As I sit in my office each week, I sometimes wish I had the power to change history for other people too. I wish I could erase the hurt, the abuse, the bad memories. I wish I could bring back the lost loved one, restore the marriage relationship, change the choices made by an errant child. That power is not mine, of course. I can't fix any of those things. What I can do is to point those who are willing to the One who can heal, reconcile, lift up.

Recently I spent part of a weekend with a dear young friend of mine who grew up with my children in Hong Kong. Her name is Rachel and she is a master potter. I knew her as a little child, sweet, innocent, and loving. As a teenager she became rebellious toward her parents and the Lord, and she began to make choices that led her to places where she did not want to be. As she works with the clay at the potter's wheel, she tells how she came back to the Father and she illustrates how He lovingly took her life apart and remade it into a vessel He could use. As I listen to her story, observe her serene manner, and watch as she mothers her children so well, I give thanks with her for what the Master Potter has done. And what He has done for her, He can do for all. We must present ourselves to Him daily and submit to His reshaping and His editing. And we must continue to share with others that there is a Person who can do this in our lives.

Approval

 $\mathcal{A}$ s you know, I have a love-hate relationship with my computer. I love it because it allows me to receive messages quickly from distant places, to see the latest antics of my grandchildren and to find information with a few taps of the keys. I hate it when it seems to have a mind of its own, when it refuses to do what I want or go where I want to go, or when those little windows pop up, insisting to be dealt with before I can continue with my online project. Sometimes, though, I feel like the Lord uses my computer to speak to me in an unexpected way. That happened recently when I opened my e-mail inbox and began to delete "spam." There in bold type I saw: "**You have been approved**."

I didn't open the message, but I continued to think about those words. So many people I see in the counseling office and whom I know in other areas are seeking approval in a variety of ways. It is quite common for men, especially, to continue to try for their father's approval, even after they are grown and he has passed away. Teenagers want the approval of their peers. Women desire the approval of their mothers and of other women. All this is very natural but can lead to some unhealthy feelings and behaviors.

In his book, <u>The Search for Significance</u>, Robert Magee lists some of the wrong thinking of approval seekers. Some think, "I must meet certain standards to feel good about myself." Others say, "I must be approved by certain others to feel good about myself." Still others feel, "Those who fail are unworthy of love and deserve to be punished." And lastly, the worst idea of all, "I am what I am and cannot change; I am hopeless." Magee makes it plain that God has a specific answer for each of these attitudes. Simply put, once we belong to Him through Christ, we do not have to fear failure, rejection, punishment or shame. To paraphrase my computer, "**We have been approved**."

I bask every day in the sunshine of my Heavenly Father's love, and I hope the same is true for you. And just to cap it off, look at what the very next e-mail message said: "**Your approval has been verified**." Read it for yourself in Romans 8:1-6.

My Friend/My Enemy

$\mathcal{F}$inally, the sun is shining! After many days of rain and grayness, today is like spring! I must tell you honestly that I don't want to be in front of my computer. I want/need to be outside pruning the plants that have been wintering on my south-facing front porch. I've been sitting here staring at this box, which has been staring back at me with its vivid blue, expressionless face. I can't help thinking of the frustration this electronic contraption has caused me recently, and of the hours I have spent on the phone with technicians guiding me through the mazes of virus quarantine and removal. I think too of the stories I am hearing each week in the counseling office of teenagers causing each other misery by telling lies in chat rooms, of men and women wounding their marriages with relationships developed on the internet, and of others who have become addicted to viewing pornography or to playing dark and dangerous games.

But then, I must think of all the ways that the computer expands and enriches my life. Just this week, due to this amazing invention, I have heard from a long lost friend, and I've had thrilling reports of what the Lord is doing in and through the lives of His servants in Indonesia, Moldova, China, Chile and Thailand. I have helped my husband send medical advice to a missionary trying to help care for a badly burned child in the country where he serves. I've received information about political and social causes that need my support. I've "chatted" with my sister about the status of our mother, who is with me. I've had messages from a couple of clients, telling me of positive happenings in their lives. And one of the nicest notes was one from my son saying he is sending us more of his music.

So I must conclude that the computer is like so many other things in life: the good or bad is not in the object itself but in how it is used. This blue-faced box is my friend, one I don't want to be without, but I'm responsible for how much time I spend with it and for where I go with it. Right now I'm bidding it goodbye and heading out into the sunshine with my pruning shears.

Other Ways

Be Still

One reference I checked today reported that more than sixty percent of adults in the U.S. are over-weight. Isn't that an astounding statistic? There are many reasons why this is so, but to state it simply, we eat too much and exercise too little. We sit in front of computers and TV sets.   We celebrate and reward ourselves and others with food. And this way of life is to our detriment. We would do well to be more active and teach our children to do so.   Strangely enough, however, I want to write today about the value of be-ing still. I don't mean "still" as in lying on the couch watching soap operas or late- night movies. I mean being purposely passive, waiting and watching to see what God will do. I am a mother, a grandmother, a counselor and a teacher who comes from a long line of strong Christian women. When trouble comes in my life or in the life of someone near me, I automatically think there must be something I can do to help. What I am learning is that sometimes the best thing I can do is to step back and give God a chance to do His work. This doesn't mean I turn my back on the situation. I am to pray and to wait in living stillness born of trust in Him.

I often meet with clients who are very agitated because of some event in their lives. They want to know WHAT TO DO. Of course, there are situations which call for action, but there are also experiences which God wants to use in our lives to teach us a personal lesson about His power. Hannah Whitehall Smith writes, "In order to know God, inner stillness is absolutely necessary." She tells of a time when an emergency occurred in her life and every part of her being throbbed with anxiety. Then she remembered God's word, *"Be still and know that I am God."* She made her body be still and her spirit be quiet; she waited. Then she "knew" His presence and had strength to deal with the emergency.

Please try to get some exercise as often as possible, but remember too how important it is to be still each day before the Lord. His word promises, *"In quietness and confidence is your strength."* Isaiah 30:15

Work in Progress

𝒯hrough our breakfast room window we have been watching the construction of two new houses. One is only at the beginning stage, with its foundation poured on soil built high to keep the house safe from floods. The other is much further along, and we have enjoyed watching, speculating and commenting as the carpenters, roofers and bricklayers have come day after day to follow the designer's plan. What a pleasure it must be for him to watch his vision become reality as each of those workmen does his assigned task.

As I've watched those houses going up, I've seen a comparison with our lives. The Great Designer has a plan of just how He wants them to look. The workmen who make it happen are the many varied experiences we have every day. They work on different parts of our "structure," and they are all needed to bring the plan to completion. And like the houses I'm watching, some of the most important work will be done on the inside where casual observers won't be able to see.

Leading my Bible Study class through the book of Ephesians, I've been reminded again that as Christians we are a *"building being fitted together to become a holy temple in the Lord, in whom we are being built together for a dwelling place of God in the Spirit."* (Eph. 2:21-22) As I meet with people in counseling, I try to help them to see that our lives are not random or without purpose, but that the circumstances they are dealing with are part of a big plan, and that the Designer is on site every day to direct the work in progress and to encourage those who are working to complete a building that will please and honor Him.

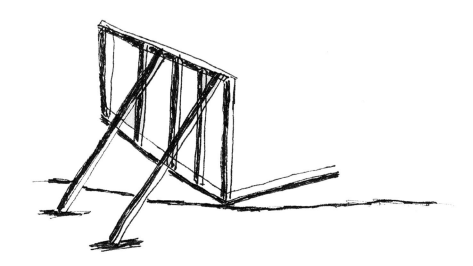

Do You Want to Be Made Well?

"Do you want to be made well?" I've been thinking about those words since I heard them on Sunday in a sermon based on the story of Jesus' visit to the pool of Bethesda. Among the many sick people gathered there to wait the stirring of the waters was a man who had been ill for *thirty-eight years*! I have lots of questions about that man: what was his disease; how old was he; didn't he have any friends or relatives who could have helped him get into the pool quickly, and if not, why not?

Jesus had a question about him, too. And as usual, His query cut right to the heart of the matter. Knowing the man had been ill for almost four decades, Jesus asked, *"Do you want to be made well?"* Amazingly, the invalid didn't answer with a resounding, "Yes!" His reply was an excuse, using words that conveyed an attitude of "poor me." (Could that be one reason he had no companions?)

Of course, I do not have the miraculous power to heal people, but my purpose in the counseling office is to help them to move into the realm of emotional, spiritual, mental and physical health. And I have to say, there are times when my question to the client *du jour* could well be, "Do you want to be well?" Not everyone who comes to counseling is really serious about it. There are teenagers who have been brought, under duress, by their parents. There is the marriage partner who has already given up on the relationship and has begun to move on. There are spouses who come together, but who each spend their counseling session trying to show me how wrong their partner is. Some individuals claim to want help with a problem they have been dealing with for a long time, but every suggestion I make is greeted with, "But I..." Here's one thing I know: Folks don't change until it becomes too uncomfortable for them to stay like they are and until they are willing to take some responsibility for their own circumstances.

Jesus came to give us abundant life. When we stop acting like victims and making excuses and get ready to make the changes that will move us closer to who He wants us to be and what He wants to give us, He stands ready to use His power in our behalf.

The Importance of Names

$\mathcal{T}$hanks to YouTube, my husband and I enjoy watching our grandchildren as they learn to sit up, feed themselves and take their first steps. Recently we were able to hear two-year-old Ellis Grace say her whole name for the first time. "Ellith Grath Langford," she lisped into the camera, smiling with pride afterward. Now she can declare to the whole world who she is!

We are all identified by our names, and they're important to us. We're pleased when people remember them, and we love to hear them spoken by those who are dear to us. I do have to wonder sometimes, however, what the parents were thinking of when certain appellations were chosen. We've all heard of the famous Hogg family in Texas, with girls named Ima and Ura. In Hong Kong I knew a young woman named Polyester Chu. In our family we name children after those who have gone before them, hoping the child will emulate the traits of that person. Both my husband and I are named for grandparents whom we greatly admired. All of our children and their children carry the name of an ancestor, so their name not only identifies them, but also places them securely in the family circle.

In biblical times, and in some cultures even today, each person's name has a meaning. Remember how significant it was that God Himself told Abram he was to be known as Abraham? And how Jesus changed Simon into Peter, the rock? If we give nick-names to our friends and children, they need to be names that describe something positive about them, a name that speaks affection, or something for them to strive toward.

The most important name any of us can bear is that of Christian. How thankful I am that I carry that personal identification as part of the family of God, one of His children. How precious to me are the words of Isaiah 43:1: *"Fear not, for I have redeemed you; I have called you by name. You are mine."*

Thanks for the Memories

𝒯his week I had one of those "voice from the past" experiences, and it was such a blessing. We don't always enjoy such calls. Don't you hate the ones that start with the cheery demand, "Guess who this is?" Sometimes calls come which remind us of people and events that we are not happy to remember. Or someone we briefly met calls to ask us to do a favor or to contribute to his pet cause. But the call I received on Monday wasn't like that. The caller told me right up front who he was, adding that I might not remember him. I'm sure it's been twenty years or more since I've seen him or heard from him, but I immediately pictured him in my mind's eye. He was a handsome Chinese teenager who attended our church and spent time with our family in Hong Kong. Age-wise, he slots in somewhere among our older children. His English name was Paul, and we all enjoyed him. He left Hong Kong later to study, and we lost touch with him.

He said he'd been thinking about the people who had influenced his life in positive ways, and that our family kept coming to mind. He decided that he needed to find us to say thank you. (It was a little disconcerting to know he located me in about thirty minutes by putting "Mary Langford," "Baptist," and Louisiana" into

Google.) We had a lovely conversation, catching up briefly on each other's life and exchanging addresses. He was gracious in his comments about me and our family and what we had meant to him. As he spoke, it was as if I was receiving a benediction from the Lord, a blessing for words and deeds long ago spoken, done and forgotten. That phone call has buoyed me up all week.

Now, whose spirits would be lifted by a call or a note from you? Is there a teacher or an older relative, a long-ago friend or a minister, someone who made a difference in your life at a crucial time, maybe without even realizing it? Wouldn't this be a great time to tell them so? To do so will make you feel good, will bless that person and will please the Lord. Go for it!

The Power of Prayer

$\mathcal{L}$ike many of you I have been watching the battles that have been taking place in Iraq during the past few weeks. It's been amazing to see the "real time" actions of our troops as they have steadily moved to take over vital cities and other important areas. But while our soldiers have been fighting their way to and through Baghdad, I've been involved in some battles, too. Don't worry, I don't own a gun, much less a weapon of mass destruction. My only weapon is prayer, and I am more and more impressed with its power and with my responsibility to learn all I can about its use.

In my first meeting with each counseling client I promise three things: to observe confidentiality, to walk with them in their difficulty, and to pray for them. As I keep these promises, I see changes occur that only God could bring about. Often I ask the clients themselves to pray for the one they see as the "troublemaker" in their lives. Usually they resist, but as they begin to try, they find that it is very hard to pray for someone and stay angry with them. Very often, circumstances are not made different by prayer, but change occurs in the one who prays.

More and more I am impelled to pray. More and more I understand that I cannot fix things, I cannot change people, I must not manipulate situations. All of that is God's job. My part is to pray. I know individuals who are in great spiritual struggles. I cannot fight their battle directly, but I can uphold them in prayer. I can give minimal comfort to those who grieve, but I pray for the Comforter to be present in the dark and lonely hours. I cannot rein in a rebellious teen-ager, but I can lift that one to the Father for His correction. I see prayer as very underused and mainly unexplored. Christ Himself prayed and He commands us to pray. Let's spend less time talking, less energy doing, and more effort practicing the use of this powerful weapon.

Take Care of the Temple

$\mathcal{I}$ often see a sign outside a chiropractor's office which asks, "If you don't take care of your body, where are you going to live?" I smile at the question, but it makes a very good point. Does it bother you, as it does me, that sixty-five percent of adults in the United States are overweight or frankly obese? When we look at the average American lifestyle, it's not hard to see how this came to be true. Because there are so many wives and mothers who work outside the home, the family meal has become almost a thing of the past. People eat grab-and-go breakfasts, skip lunch or get fat-and-carb-loaded fast food, and pick up pizza or fried chicken to take home for supper. And we sit in front of the computer, behind a desk, in front of the TV.

Most of us are not lazy. We work hard to earn a living and to care for our families. Those of you who read this are active in your church, always ready to lend a helping hand. But how well are we taking care of ourselves? How many of us help to make up the ominous sixty-five percent? If we truly believe that our bodies are the temple of His spirit, how are we taking care of His dwelling place? And does that have anything to do with our witness to those who don't know the Lord?

I've never been a great athlete, but in recent years I've become a real proponent of exercise. It's a strong suggestion I make to almost every counseling client, because I've observed in others and experienced myself the good effects mentally and physically. If you don't have at least a moderate exercise plan in action, I urge you to begin one. And I urge you to discuss with your family the need to eat healthily, and then begin supporting each other in doing just that: lots more fresh fruits, vegetables, lean meat and healthy snacks. Lots less high fat, high carbohydrate stuff. Help your children to form eating habits that will benefit them for a lifetime. Take time to sit together and talk as you eat. If you don't take care of your body, where are you going to live?

Keeping Relationships in Repair

$\mathcal{I}$ am ever at war against entropy! The engineers out there will know that this is the law which describes the tendency of everything to move from order to disorder. A new car depreciates the moment you drive it off the lot. A freshly cleaned kitchen will stay that way about five minutes, max. Faucets begin to drip. Weeds grow in flower beds. Toys and newspapers are strewn around the living room. Hips and knees need to be replaced. You fight entropy too, don't you?

The same principle that governs the tendency toward disorder and disintegration also applies in human relationships. Friendships must be maintained in much the same way that we tend to a garden. Partners in a marriage will drift apart unless they intentionally employ the directions in scripture to cherish, nurture, love and respect each other. That means deliberately taking time for activities and experiences that draw them together. It may be just talking a few minutes a day, really connecting with each other over a cup of coffee or during a walk.

Children will wander and drift away, especially during the teen years, unless special effort is made to make them feel an important part of a permanent circle. An interesting study recently revealed many long-term benefits in the lives of children whose families had regular meals together as a simple forum for talking, listening, observing, encouraging.

We spend so much of our time cleaning and maintaining our houses and yards, doing jobs we are paid to do, feeding our bodies. Are we aware every day of the need and the responsibility we have to maintain our relationships? It may take something as simple as a hug or a phone call, a note in a lunch-box or a briefcase. Maybe a child needs a Saturday morning breakfast with Dad. Maybe Dad needs a back rub, or a wife would enjoy an evening out. We will drift apart unless we use purposeful energy to stay together.

This morning I mailed a note to a friend to congratulate him on his daughter's accomplishment. On the way back from the mailbox I stopped to weed a flower bed. Ever at war against entropy! Join me in the battle!

Mindfulness

Some time ago I received training in a program called "Zest for Life," which is designed to help senior citizens continue to enjoy life while aging. One of the emphases in the program is that of "awareness", being very mindful of each moment as you live in it, not looking back to yesterday or last year, or day-dreaming of things to come, just treasuring each moment as it comes. I decided to purposely "be aware" today as I spent much of the day working in my kitchen. I set myself the task of replacing the shelf paper and straightening all the shelves, sorting through dishes and getting rid of things I don't use. At first I thought I could listen to a Christian radio station as I worked, but I quickly decided to choose silence so that I might more easily hear anything the Lord might communicate to me in the midst of my mundane task.

And you know what? It worked. All day long my thoughts were guided by Him. He showed me things I didn't need and suggested who I might share them with. As I straightened and discarded, He reminded me that is what He is always doing in my life: working on the inside where others may not see or know. That old shelf paper was hard to remove, but I kept after it till I had disposed of all of it and replaced it with new and clean.

The Father reminded me of a verse, and I kept repeating it back to Him, *"Create in me a clean heart, O God."*

Certain items reminded me of the person who had given them to us, and I could thank the Lord for the blessing of friendship. I set aside some picnic plates and pretty coffee mugs to offer to our daughter, and took some time to pray for her and her family, those precious grandsons. When I stopped for lunch, I was very aware of how easy it was for me to find the fixings for a tasty sandwich. I stopped to ask God's mercy on those who never have enough to eat.

I had a very special day. No TV, no radio, just the Lord and me working together in my kitchen. I think this is a touch of what Brother Lawrence calls "practicing the presence of Christ." I recommend it to you: silence, purposeful awareness, being with Him in the moment, learning lessons from mundane tasks. I will choose it again soon. I'm not yet finished with my kitchen, and I know He's not finished with me.

The Old Plow

*A*t our house we are on a campaign to go through closets and storage areas, sort and straighten things, and get rid of what we don't need. I'm thinking that if we continue to work at it during most of our "free" time, we will probably complete the job right around my ninetieth birthday. Those of you who have done this sort of thing know that in the process you come across some strange items that cause you to wonder what you were thinking when you bought them or why you have kept them. One reason the task is so slow is because we need to stop to read old notes and letters, or relive the memories brought back by a packet of forgotten photographs. Or we must stop and discuss/debate the usefulness of something that one wants and the other thinks should be delivered to Goodwill.

One of the most unusual items we have stashed away is a heavy, wooden, very old plow used long ago to prepare rice fields in China. We bought it on impulse from another missionary years ago in Hong Kong. It was crudely handmade and the dark wood scarred from long use. I think it appealed to us because it symbolized so well the hard work and patience that have always characterized the Chinese people. We weren't sure what we would do with it. One idea we had was to hang it on a wall framing the words of Luke 9:62. We never did that, but when we left Hong Kong, we brought the old implement with us to Lafayette where it gathers dust in storage.

That plow is about not quitting, not giving up. Every week I talk with people who are ready to do that. Ministers and wives are weary of the trials of church leadership. Husbands or wives are considering divorce. Some folks find their job situations to be intolerable. The saddest are those who feel that life itself is not worth living. My job is to offer encouragement, and to try to point to a hopeful path.

The last verses of Luke 9 are about the cost of discipleship. Jesus calls people to follow Him and they make excuses. Finally He says, *"No one, having put his hand to the plow and looking back, is fit for the kingdom of God."* Just a reminder, my friends, that our Lord expects and honors faithfulness. If you come to my house and see an old plow on the wall, you'll know what it means.

Livin' in Fast Forward

$\mathcal{I}$ can't recall whether I have confessed to you my love of country music. It's not that I like every song or all the ideas, but a lot of them have catchy tunes and lyrics that are funny, clever and even profound. I won't take the time and space here to review some of my favorites, but one I heard recently fits right in with my thoughts for this month. Kenny Chesney sings, "I'm livin' in fast forward, needin' to rewind real slow." Can't you relate to that? I can.

Since I wrote last, we've all had Christmas and New Year, and I've had a birthday. By the time you read this, I'll have a brand-new granddaughter! Already we're looking at February and the next big event or celebration. My mail is full of upcoming deadlines and opportunities. Every day has its own "to-do." list. Life moves swiftly, and happenings overlap so that we cannot fully absorb or enjoy one before the next one is upon us.

Having another birthday and starting a new year have prompted me to determine that, whenever possible, I will slow my pace. I want to watch for windows of time, little islands for rest and reflection. I want to take in colors, be aware of fragrances, look into eyes, smile at people, feel the sun's warmth, savor my food, hear the words of songs. I hope to be fully present to everyone I converse with. I look forward to holding that new baby close with her fingers curled around mine. I want to just sit with the Lord, aware of His presence, not asking for anything, waiting for His word to me. Does any of this sound inviting to you?

I think Kenny Chesney has the right idea. The Psalmist put it this way: *"Teach us to number our days that we may obtain a heart of wisdom."*

East Meets West

$\mathcal{I}$ wish you could have been with us last weekend when my husband and I went to Memphis for a wedding. The son of Chinese friends was marrying an American girl, and the event disproved the saying that East and West never meet. Several things about the ceremony were unusual: There were no flowers, no bridesmaids, no groomsmen. The bride's mother and father walked her down the aisle as the young groom played a beautiful melody on the violin. Then the couple stood facing the congregation under a bright red Chinese arch to hear the pastor's words and to recite vows they had written. Both bride and groom were barefoot. The reception definitely presented the best of both worlds with a bountiful spread of Chinese and American delicacies, American music, and an old-fashioned Chinese tea ceremony. In the midst of all the mix of old and new, oriental and occidental, no doubt was left in anyone's mind that these two people loved the Lord and each other and were serious (and very happy) about the ceremony and celebration which marked the beginning of their life together.

I think Jesus was present at that wedding, as much as He was at the one where He performed the first miracle. And I believe He enjoyed them both.

Although He never married, it seems that Jesus gave a lot of thought to marriage and spoke of it several times in the New Testament. Most interesting is that He referred to Himself as the Bridegroom, with the church as His bride. I understand the Ephesians 5 passage to be saying that when a man and woman marry, their union is to present to the world a picture of Christ and the church. How many people are aware of that on their wedding day? As the Divine Husband, Christ loved the church and gave Himself for it. And the church is to respond in loving and grateful service, following His lead. I often go through that scripture with couples in the counseling office, pointing out God's instruction to the husband to love, nourish and cherish his wife, and the wife to respect her husband. I encourage them to spend their life together learning what that means. Asian or Western, barefoot or in shoes, I think that's what the Inventor of marriage had in mind.

Ways to Remember

My husband and I say that between the two of us we have one memory. We'll start talking about a person or a place and get stuck on the name. We struggle with it a bit, then try to move on. Later, sometimes hours later, one of us will suddenly come up with it, and our minds are at ease—until we can't remember something else. I don't think we're alone in this. I hear other people talking about memory loss, or joking about having Alzheimer's disease. Those of us who have lived with an Alzheimer's patient know it's not a laughing matter. We can, however, relate to the frustration, and maybe the bit of fear, that comes with loss of memory.

Something I read this week caused me to think of what God forgets and what He remembers. His word tells us that He buries our sins and remembers them no more. Isn't it wonderful to know that the Father is not keeping a list of offenses which He can use against us at any time?

There are many times when God does remember. The Bible says He remembered Noah and his family in the ark, He remembered Hannah and gave her a son. Jesus promised to remember the thief dying on the cross. I'm sure this doesn't mean He suddenly recalled where they were or what they needed or had requested. It's not the same as when we remember where we put our car keys. No, God's remembering always involved love in action, more in the way we remember our mothers on Mother's Day or veterans on Memorial Day, doing something to honor them, to show they are important to us.

In my office I see so many folks who are carrying burdens of hurtful memories. Often they will say they cannot/will not forgive the one who has caused so much pain. Their lives are constricted because of what they choose to keep in the forefront of their memory. Sometimes they use that memory as a weapon to hurt others. Would that we could all ask the Lord to help us to be willing to bury past offenses and to choose to remember in the way He does—with acts of love, kindness and encouragement.

His By Adoption

𝒯his spring I became aware of a family who has opened their home on a long-term basis to five children and a mother. I learned of another couple who have taken in a special needs child whom they are rearing as their own. Only the Lord can know what the selflessness and generosity of these people will mean for the future of these little ones who are so precious to Him.

I know many young couples who have chosen to adopt one or more children who have been left without a parent. This week we met one such pair who are happily getting acquainted with their new little Chinese daughter. How different her life will be because of the love and the opportunities that this new relationship will provide her. We returned home to find an urgent message from another couple, asking for help in deciding about the adoption of a child with special needs. How wonderful that they are even willing to consider taking on this kind of lifetime challenge!

All this has caused me to review the stories of some of the adoptees I've worked with in counseling. In almost every case, there is an inexpressible sense of being not quite complete, of not quite belonging, no matter how loving their adoptive parents have been. I recall once hearing a man tell that as a teenager he had learned that he was adopted. His world was shattered; he felt totally lost. Who was he? Whom could he trust? Then someone told him about the Heavenly Father's plan of making us into His children. He came into that relationship and lived confidently as the son of a faithful, unchanging Father.

Are we not all orphans, incomplete, looking for the place where we belong? What a blessing when we come to understand and accept the words in Ephesians 1:3: *"Blessed be the God and Father of our Lord Jesus Christ, who has blessed us with every spiritual blessing in the heavenly places in Christ, just as in Him before the foundation of the world, that we should be holy and without blame before Him in love, having predestined us to adoption as sons by Jesus Christ to Himself, according to the pleasure of His good will, to the praise and glory of His grace, by which He has made us accepted in the Beloved."* How different and blessed our lives are because we are adopted!

Walking My Street

$\mathcal{L}$ike many of you, I resolved again this year to get more exercise. So, in the cool and sunny weather we've been having, I've put on my walking shoes and headed out. Five laps around my one-street subdivision is two miles. Now, as we all know, one needs to walk briskly in order to increase heart rate and burn more calories. I'm sure the Lord wants me to take good care of my body, but lately I'm finding it almost impossible to make those five laps without being interrupted. One day I reached the house on the front corner to find its owner, a young mother, by her mailbox. What I meant to be a quick greeting turned out to be a conversation in which I learned that she and her husband are separated. Of course, I offered my help and my prayers. Recently I was clipping along at a really good pace when the widow from across the main road walked over just to chat and let me know her house is for sale. We talked of how she's managing since her husband's death.

My most delightful "interrupter," however, is the beautiful little five-year-old girl who lives with her grandmother in the third house up from ours. She and her two younger sisters have dark curly hair, dark eyes and captivating smiles. Invariably, if I walk in the afternoon, little Miss Five-year-old comes running to join me. I need to walk fast, but she can't keep up, so I slow my pace to hers. She puts her hand in mine and we walk and talk for as many laps as she is able. I've learned which school she attends and that blue is her favorite color. She said she and her sisters sleep in the same room. On Wednesday she said, "Tonight is garbage night. And we'll go dumpster diving!" Then she declared, "My daddy's in jail. He'll get out in fifteen days. Then he said he'd come meet me at the bus-stop after school." As our walk ended, I said I had a little gift for her. She didn't say, "What is it?" but only, "Can my sisters have some too?"

Here's what I think God is teaching me through the people on my street: our agendas need to be flexible enough to allow time to enter into the lives of others. Maybe no one else is stopping to listen or to offer to pray. I do need to walk fast, but maybe I need to be willing to make a couple of extra laps to offset the times I stopped. What could possibly be more precious or important than walking slower while holding the hand of a little dumpster diver? And please Lord, help her daddy keep his bus-stop promise.

Love With No Strings

This morning I talked with a long-time friend. I don't quite understand why our friendship has lasted so long, as we actually have very little in common. She is Jewish and very wealthy. She and her husband jet back and forth between their two homes, a big "flat" in Hong Kong and a newly decorated apartment in Manhattan. They seem to have no interest in spiritual things. Her stay in the States will be prolonged this time because she has just begun chemotherapy for treatment of recently diagnosed Hodgkin's Lymphoma. We talk more often now, and she seems to appreciate my calls. She was touched when I offered to go to be with her for a while. When I told her I was praying for her, she thanked me, but moved quickly on. He defenses are very strong, and I've never been able to penetrate them.

I see other versions of this in the counseling office. Some people come for help, but when they realize they would have to face their own mistakes or sin and be open to change, they bolster their defenses and stop coming to see me.

Sometimes people just don't want what we have to offer. We shouldn't be surprised. That was true for

Jesus too, wasn't it? Remember the rich young ruler, and how many scribes and Pharisees and common people? Our job, as I see it, is to offer love as Christ has given so graciously to us, and then to continue to love, whether the person accepts or not.

Although it seems to mean nothing to her, I will continue to pray for my friend. I am not the only instrument God has. I am asking Him to somehow communicate Himself to her during this life battle. And I also try to pray that way for those who come for counseling but are not ready to change.

Old Letters

The last assignment of this semester in my Life Writing class involves letters. We were to bring old letters to share or to write a letter to read to the group. The old letters were wonderful to hear. A lady in her eighties read a formal and flowery letter written in 1910 by her father to her mother before they married. Another octogenarian shared the loving words written to her by her father when she was eight years old, such a treasure. A third classmate read aloud the words of admiration and appreciation sent to her by her daughters on her birthday, better than any material gift. As I listened to the letters I felt that I knew something of the writers. They were expressing themselves.

In counseling when a person is working through a difficulty in a past or present relationship, I often suggest that he or she write a letter to the other person. It may or may not be mailed, but writing the letter often promotes mental and emotional healing.

Christ came to earth in human form, the arrival of God's best expression of Himself to the world. John said it plainly in John 1:1,14: *"In the beginning was the Word and the Word was with God. And the Word, was made flesh, and dwelt among us, and we beheld His glory, the glory of the only begotten of the Father, full of grace and truth."*

How fortunate we are to have received this letter of love and healing?

Lord, Do You See Me?

In October I attended the Great Commission Prayer Conference, as did many of you. It was such a blessing to me, the message by Lewis Drummond, the meaningful workshops, the worship times with wonderful music, the fellowship with other believers. And I so enjoyed hearing the energetic and inspiring John Avant. In his Saturday morning message he told of being somewhere in Asia on a mission trip a month ago. It was a dangerous location due to government restrictions. He spoke of the fear he felt, especially when he realized that no one at home knew where he was and that he himself didn't really know. Then he said he heard the Lord whisper in his ear, "*I know where you are.*"

When he told that story, I recalled experiences and feelings from my years in Hong Kong. Often I would be on a bus, a subway train, or a crowded street, and I would realize that I was the only Westerner in a great mass of Chinese people. All around me were black-eyed, black-haired Asians speaking in languages other than English. Sometimes I would silently whisper to God, "Lord, do you see me down here? Do you know where I am?" And He always assured me with a smile, *"Yes, my dear, I surely do."*

Every week in the counseling office I meet with people who are lonely or grieving, with those who have been mistreated by those who should have protected them. I talk with people who are struggling in difficult relationships or with unhealthy desires. I sit with those who are trying to put the pieces of their lives back together, having suffered the consequences of their own or someone else's choices. I am so thankful that I can give to them the comforting word that they are not alone, but that God knows where they are. Not only does He know their location, but He is the map-maker, and He will walk with them every step of the road they must take. I point them to Psalm 139 and to Jeremiah 29:11. Read those passages again this week for yourself, and hear the Father saying to you, *"My dear child, be assured I always know where you are."*

Morgan's Question

Years ago I knew a bright and funny little boy named Morgan. Several of our family sayings stem from things we heard him say as a small child. Recently I've been reminded of a burning question I once heard Morgan ask. I was walking with some other adults down a roadway at an encampment, and Morgan was following us. It was evening time, and the limited lighting caused our shadows to fall behind us. As the grown-ups chatted with one another, Morgan followed us quietly, thinking his own thoughts. Suddenly, a loud cry erupted from the little boy as he wailed, "Where's MY shadow?" Apparently, he had been walking along behind us, seeing our shadows, but unable to see his own. We laughed and tried to explain to him, but I never forgot his pained question.

Sometimes people come into my counseling office with the same concern that Morgan had. In different words from his, they are asking, "Does my life matter?" "Do I have any influence for good?" "Is my work worthwhile?" In the last few months I have heard this query in some form from some of the most dedicated workers in the churches of our association. In each case I've tried to share with them an assurance that came to me some years ago from the pen of Elisabeth Elliot. At the close of <u>A CHANCE TO DIE</u>, her biography of Amy Carmichael, she says:

"Our enemy whispers, 'Where are the proofs? Let's have statistics.' We may and we must look at the visible, but let us remember that there is far more to be taken into account. What we can see doesn't tell the whole story. The gold, silver, and precious stones may be in safe deposit where we can't get at them. We may draw up a list of known results, but our criteria are restricted. Some are visible. God knows the rest. None but He knows the steadiness of obedience, the unseen struggle, the hidden offerings, the quality of faith."

May I assure you, as we did Morgan years ago, don't worry, you do have a shadow, even when you can't see it.

For Those Who Cannot Speak

One of my pet peeves is for someone to make an appointment with me for counseling and then not show up. When that happens, a time slot is left vacant that another person could have used, and I lose the fee. Today I felt more than the usual regret as I waited for a client who did not come. She had been referred to me by the Crisis Pregnancy Center because she was struggling with the decision as to whether to have an abortion. She never arrived, I didn't meet with her, and I fear what that might mean about the choice she has made. She may have made a choice that is made very commonly in our country today ever since that famous court case which championed a women's "Right to Choose."

We are all still dealing with the enormity of the event of September 11 when 5000 or more people died. Are you aware that for the last many years any date could be substituted for September 11 and the number of the death toll would still be correct? Every day in this land of the free and home of the brave, 5000 unborn children are put to death. The grim total registers in the millions. As we think of Osama Bin

Laden and the need to bring him to justice for his part in terrorist acts against our country, don't we need to consider the beam in our own eye?

As American Christians we must do all we can to strengthen our own family relationships. We must teach our children openly and in a positive way about sexuality, about self-respect and respect for others, about abstinence. We must spend enough time with the young people in our families to know what is going on in their lives and who their friends are. We need to be sure that they know they can talk to us about anything, bring to us any problem and be assured of our love and our help. As citizens of this most blessed land, we must speak out and stand against the daily killing of little ones who have no voice. And in our churches we must offer forgiveness and restoration to those who regret their part in ending such a life. We are responsible before the Lord for what has been done, and for what we now do to keep it from continuing.

We Can Choose

A week ago workmen came along and completely tore up the road between my house and Johnston Street. Then they brought in loads of dirt and spread it around. Then came the lime. Then more dirt. Then they went away, and we haven't seen them since. The road is now either muddy or dusty and is like driving on a wash board. You know what else? The weeds and grass are growing high in my yard, and the person who's supposed to mow it has not appeared. A lifelong friend of mine in California has just learned that she has cancer. Another friend in New York has severe heart problems. My husband has been on call for his job for the last three weekends in a row. I'd have to drive seven hours to see my nearest child, and my only grandchild lives a thousand miles away.

But you know what else is true? It's strawberry season, and we can have those luscious red berries morning, noon, and night, which I'm sure is what the Lord intends. It's also true that the azaleas and dogwoods are blooming all over town, shouting at us as we go by. And I received a thank you note today from the mother of a young woman I am trying to help. And as far as I know, I'm in excellent health. And my California friend is feeling good in spite of the chemo treatments. My mother who's in a retirement center has a positive attitude. My husband has a job. I have meaningful work to do. Do you see where I'm going with this? WE CAN CHOOSE WHAT WE THINK AND TALK ABOUT.

Often I see in the counseling office someone who is depressed or who feels that their life is "stuck." Or maybe I will see a couple whose relationship has become stagnant. One of the suggestions I make to such persons is that they begin to make written lists of anything in their day they see that is beautiful, or funny, or encouraging, and that they share their lists with others each evening. They find that just trying to fulfill this assignment makes them much more alert to flowers and sunsets and music, to smiles and friendliness, to many of the little blessings in life that they had failed to notice. Try it. Buy a little spiral notebook for everybody in your family and ask them to make a "good" list every day to be shared with the rest of the family once or twice a week. Teach each other to lift up on your corner of the world.

The best psychological advice ever given is found in Philippians 4:8: *"Finally brethren, whatsoever things are true, whatsoever things are honest, whatsoever things are just, whatsoever things are pure, whatsoever things are lovely, whatsoever things are of good report; if there be any virtue, if there be any praise, think on these things."*

Use what You Have

My children and I like to play games, and I especially enjoy a good game of Scrabble. I've now been introduced to Facebook, by which I can play the game with people who are miles away. I'm presently involved in two games online and one at home with a daughter and a daughter-in-law. As we all know, there is some knowledge and experience involved, but a great deal depends on the tiles drawn by each player. If my opponent draws the X, the Z, the Q, the J and such, and I have only one-point letters, my chances of prevailing are greatly diminished. And yet, I must play the tiles I've drawn, trying to make the highest score of which they are capable.

Another thing my daughter-in-law and I do together is to have a long-distance Bible study. Right now we're studying the lives of certain women who lived in biblical times. This week's study centers around Leah, the weak-eyed elder sister of Rachel. As you recall, Rachel was very beautiful, and Jacob loved her right away, gladly working the seven years her father required of him. But, through trickery, Leah became Jacob's first wife. She bore him six sons and a daughter, hoping in vain for his love. Although she never attained the desire of her heart, she found her value in God's sight. She never became Jacob's favorite, but after the birth of each child, she praised God, continuing to trust Him. Leah didn't blame the Lord for her disappointing and hurtful circumstances, and she was loving to her husband and children.

In games and in life, we might not have the beauty, advantages, tools or acceptance which seems to be enjoyed by others more favored. We may be surrounded by negative circumstances of our own or another's making. We may not live to see our dreams fulfilled. We may be rejected by one who is very dear to us. We can and we must, however, do all we can with what comes to us, always trusting the One who has the master plan, and thanking Him for every good gift, although its form may not be as we had hoped. Leah did not know that Judah, one of her six sons, would be the ancestor of the Messiah. We cannot imagine what God will make of the pain-tinged efforts we offer to Him.

About the Author

Mary Langford is a Licensed Professional Counselor who has lived and worked in Lafayette, Louisiana, since 1990. For twenty-six years prior to that time, she and her physician husband were missionaries in Hong Kong where their five children grew up. She is the author of two other books: *Songs in a Strange Land* and *That Nothing Be Wasted.*